Clowning from the Heart

One Smile at a Time

CLOWNING FROM THE HEART
One Smile at a Time

The design elements of this book were produced with the help of AI.

BIBLE SCRIPTURES

Published in the United States of America by

Spirit Media and our logos are trademarks of
Spirit Media Publishing
205 S Academy St #3251
Cary, NC 27519-3251
1 (888) 800-3744 | https://spiritmedia.us

Religion & Spirituality | Christian Living | Devotional

Paperback ISBN: 979-8-89307-224-2
eBook ISBN: 979-8-89307-225-9
PDF ISBN: 979-8-89307-226-6
Library of Congress Control Number: 2026903169

Dedication

I would like to dedicate this book to my amazing children and grandchildren.

To my incredible son, David, and my beautiful daughter, Jennifer: may you always find joy and laughter in your hearts. I am so proud of you both.
All my love,
Mom

To my very talented grandchildren, Kyle, Seth, Kayla, and Cody: I am so proud of each one of you. Always follow your dreams and never stop reaching for the stars.
All my love,
"Little G"

Table of Contents

FOREWORD

Who is Sparkle?

Hi, my name is Sparkle, and I am a clown. You see, I'm not just any clown, I am a gospel clown. Many of you might wonder, "What is a gospel clown?" To me, a gospel clown is a clown who loves the Lord with all of his or her heart and loves all people as well.

I like to believe that my love for the Lord is as strong and genuine as it could possibly be. Throughout my life, I have been through many trials physically, emotionally, and spiritually. I have been tried in fire many times over and have come out shining as bright as gold. I love all people, young and old, and I want people to know how special they are just by being themselves.

Sparkle is an entity that takes the form of a beautiful clown. She represents safety, security, honesty, compassion, hope, and, above all, love.

My mission is to encourage and show the love of the Lord to people and to let them feel how beautiful and special they are inside and out. I also want to put smiles on the faces of all people everywhere. There are people of all ages who suffer from loneliness, fear, anxiety, illnesses, and physical ailments. Then there is the stress that life can bring to one every day.

So if I can put a smile on someone's face, even if for a short period of time, then I have accomplished my mission.

I do this by entertaining and teaching kids through humor, skits, storytelling, balloon animals, and sleight of hand magic with a lesson. Many times I will give a powerful message to go along with the activity. It seems that kids remember the message better this way.

The most important thing that I can do for people is to listen to them. Everyone has stories to tell, whether the stories are exciting and good, or scary and bad. The one thing that people have in common is that they all need to tell their story so that they can feel heard and valued. Sparkle is so special because through her, I am able to sit and listen to people. I want each person to know how loved and valued they truly are.

I enjoy visiting with people at hospitals, nursing homes, schools, churches, and parks, as well as being a part of festivals in the community and different local events. There are so many opportunities to share the love of the Lord, and I delight in being a part of this great journey with Sparkle.

Maya Angelou once said, "I've learned that people will forget what you said, people will forget what you did, but people will never forget how you made them feel."

Sparkle has touched the lives of thousands of people over the past few decades. I hope her story can touch you as well.

The pursuit of happiness….
is the greatest feat man has to
accomplish. –Robert Henri

CHAPTER 1

The Clown Contest

With a chance for my family to win a free trip to the sandy shores of a tropical island, my sisters and I became very interested in our town's first-ever clown contest.

In the Bible, and still today, we see the Lord calls people to do often unexpected or crazy things to further His kingdom. Think of the story of Joshua: instead of using weapons or tools, God told him to march around Jericho for a week while blowing trumpets, and the strong stone walls of the city fell. Can you imagine that type of faith? The army around Joshua must have thought that he had gone insane, but ultimately the Lord was able to use that obedience for His good. In a same, and completely different way, the Lord called me to something pretty unexpected in my life: to be Sparkle the Clown and share God's love with people. Now, after thirty-five years of being Sparkle, I can reflect on the joyful and fun memories as well as the emotional and touching moments. Thinking about this clown contest so long ago, I see how the Lord was already prompting and preparing my heart for the love of something so unexpected and unique.

It all started in my little desert town of California City. It was a small retirement town, and my family was well known because we were the only family with young children: my older sister, Cathy; my younger sister, Linda; and myself, Cindy. Our last name is Love, and so we quickly became known as the Love Kids around the neighborhood.

By the time we were in early elementary school, the town had grown to include some other young families, and the community began to have family events. One summer, around 1965 when I was about seven years old, there was a clown contest. Just about every kid in the Mojave Desert wanted to participate. There were all types of prizes, but we only wanted the prize that came with first place. The winner and their family would be brought over to a beautiful island on the S.S. *Catalina*, a very large ship, with none other than Catalina Cappy as their guide. Catalina Cappy was a well-known professional clown who was one of the original Ronald McDonald characters. Oddly enough, he was also a longtime friend of my mother. The morning of the contest, he came over to visit with my mom, meet our family, and (although he was not supposed to) he gave us kids a few pointers about the contest. We promised not to tell anyone that we had met him, because we might have been disqualified from the contest if they found out that we knew the host.

That evening you could feel the excitement in the air as all the kids from California City gathered in a long line to get on stage, covered in white and red makeup. My sisters and I were among them, dressed to our best: we had tattered and worn gloves, and we outlined our red mouths with a black makeup stick, just as Cappy had told us to.

Admittedly, standing at just a little over three feet tall, Linda was the most adorable of all of us. She dressed as a hobo clown and had a pair of big tan pants which were rolled at the bottom and held up with a belt. A huge baggy shirt, a pair of oversized boots, and a hat that sat sideways on her tiny head topped off the rest of her image.

I watched as she tripped over her boots trying to get on stage. Once she got her wobbly self on stage, Catalina Cappy, acting as the contest's MC, asked her for her name. In front of the whole town and judges, my little sister slugged Cappy on the arm. "Oh, you know my name, silly." she laughed.

My sister Cathy and I gasped, she had outed our secret to the whole town. We thought for sure that we would be disqualified. Somehow, through playful banter, they were able to play it off as a joke, and my most adorable little sister went on to win first place and the extravagant prize that came with it. My family and I got to spend a few beautiful days among swaying palm trees on Catalina Island while listening to the clowning tales of Catalina Cappy. I did not know it then, but God was planting a little seed in me, a love of clowning, that I would go on to use nearly twenty years later.

Happiness does not depend on outward things, but on the way we see them. –Leo Tolstoy

CHAPTER 2

Benji

More than two decades later, in my late twenties, I was living in Walla Walla, Washington and working in the billing department of the local hospital. I was married with two young children and had not thought about clowning since my days on the S.S. *Catalina*. As you can imagine, working in a hospital is not the most upbeat or cheery job, so when my friend Elizabeth came to me with the idea to dress up as clowns to visit patients around the hospital, I jumped at the idea. My administrator was wary, but he agreed and told me that no one had thought to do that before.

That weekend I sewed together a red-and-white patterned jumpsuit and bought my first red wig. Thankfully it was around Halloween time, so Elizabeth and I were able to go to the store for our makeup. We had no idea what we were doing, but we laughed as we put on the sticky white paint and big red noses.

The next weekend we walked around the hospital visiting patients and watching as their eyes lit up when we walked in the room. Some of them giggled for the first time since becoming a patient, and you could feel their sadness lift away for a few minutes. I had no idea what I was doing at the time. I did not have a clown name and could not craft a balloon animal, but it felt nice to laugh, tell stories, and help the patients escape their harsh reality for an afternoon.

The next week, my administrator came to me and raved about the difference he saw in the patients' emotional levels the day we visited. He excitedly told me that Elizabeth and I could do this whenever we wanted, as long as it did not interfere with work. So over the course of the next few months, Elizabeth and I would gear up and visit as many people as we could, trying to be a small light in some otherwise dark rooms.

One day, to my surprise, my supervisor came to me, desperately asking if I could go put on my clown costume. I was a little confused considering clowning was something done on my off time, but she was adamant that I needed to do it right then; there was a little child named Benji who needed my help. So I hurried home to put on my suit and makeup and headed back to the hospital.

I will never forget walking into Benji's room for the first time. He was this tiny young toddler, covered in a body cast from his chest to his toes, with terror in his little eyes. He had clearly been horribly abused, and he was scared of everyone. His mom sat nearby. Her appearance was unkempt and disheveled, and the smell of sweat and grime rose from both her and Benji. Her presence felt less maternal and more comparable to a wicked puppeteer, watching and manipulating Benji's words so that he could not get her in trouble.

Not a single doctor or nurse was able to get near Benji without him screaming and thrashing around. Even wrapped in his huge cast, he would fight them away, trying to bite them, and hurting himself more in the process. He desperately needed X-rays and further care, but he was not letting anyone get close to him.

When Benji finally saw me, I saw his little body relax for the first time. He quieted down and let me come up beside his small crib. I calmly dried his tears and smiled at him as he took it all in. Then for the first time, he smiled.

We spent the next hour together, playing and laughing, trying to forget about what brought him there in the first place. Hospital staff stopped in during that period to see the amazing transformation Benji had gone through, and at the end of our time together we got a Polaroid picture of the two of us smiling. I took a moment to appreciate it. Dressing up as a clown was so much more than just a Saturday afternoon activity; it was a beautiful gift that the Lord could use to touch the lives of those who are hurting and scared.

I gave Benji the photo to hold on to, because it was time for me to leave. Almost immediately, he started lashing out when he realized that I was not staying. The tears started flowing, but I had to go home, get cleaned up, and head back to work. As soon as work ended, I rushed to Benji's room to see him. He had reverted back to being completely terrified. He was screaming and thrashing around and did not recognize me without my clown outfit. I asked his mom if she had the Polaroid of us from earlier. She pulled it out and I quickly brought it over to show him. "I know your friend." I said, trying to be cheerful, but the screaming continued. "Benji, look. I am the clown." It took his little mind a second to connect the dots, but soon he recognized that

I was his friend, even without the makeup and red hair. He calmed down and I felt his little body relax again. He was safe.

We were inseparable after that.

For the next six weeks, I stopped by to see Benji during my breaks, lunchtimes, or even on the weekend. I even brought my kids to play with him, and I watched as they generously and excitedly shared their toys. Eventually, Benji stopped being afraid of the rest of the hospital staff, and I saw him realize that they were there to help him, not hurt him. I still remember the day he got discharged: I ran to the front of the hospital just in time to see him about to leave. I opened the door, took his little hand, and told him everything would be alright. I told him that I loved him. With a small smile and tears in his eyes, he looked at me and said, "I love you too," before his family drove off. Thankfully, although I did not know it then, I would see Benji again throughout the next few years.

Through my initial time with Benji, I realized how much good my clowning could do. I could use it to help heal the hurting, and I realized it could be more than a hobby, but my ministry. I was not quite sure what the Lord planned to do with my newfound passion, but I held on tight and was excited to watch where He would take this new joy of mine.

Happiness… leads none
of us by the same route.
–Charles Caleb Colton

CHAPTER 3

Becoming Sparkle

Every Mother's Day weekend, in my town of Walla Walla, there is a huge hot air balloon festival, Balloon Stampede. There are fun booths, a bunch of hot air balloons, and, to my enjoyment, clowns. In May of 1989, shortly after meeting Benji, I attended the Balloon Stampede with my two children, David and Jennifer. At this point, I had decided wholeheartedly that clowning would no longer be just a casual hobby; Benji made me realize it could be so much more and that if I took it seriously, it could change a lot of lives for the better. I decided to introduce myself to the clowns and see what information I could glean.

I discovered that two of the clowns I met were a mother-daughter duo: Rosemary, an Auguste Clown, and Molly, her daughter, a hobo clown. I told them about my limited time with clowning, but that I had big dreams and desires to change lives, and it turned out they had very similar values. They were both Christians and wanted to use their clowning talents to spread joy to hurting children too. Rosemary told me about a clowning workshop coming up and encouraged me to attend. I could meet other like-minded people, learn from a professional, and have fun with the community. So we exchanged numbers, and I promised to sign up for the workshop. I walked away from the encounter feeling like Christ had set up that meeting intentionally, and I was even more excited for the road ahead.

I, along with a few others including Rosemary and Molly, attended the workshop a few weekends later. It was led by a professional, Lil Petal. She started off with the history of clowning and then jumped into everyone's favorite part: the makeup. I had only ever used cheap, greasy paint from Halloween stores, and I was amazed to see what real makeup could do. I watched, on the edge of my seat, as Lil Petal transformed from an average woman to a joyful, beautiful clown.

After putting on her makeup, Lil Petal performed a moving and emotional routine titled "The Rose" by Bette Midler. By the end of it, all of us had tears rolling down our faces. I had never seen something like that before and never knew clowning could move me on such a deep level.

Now that we were all inspired, it was our turn. We each carefully put on our makeup and discussed what kind of clown we might want to be. During this time, Lil Petal paid special attention to me. She told me I had soft features that I should play up to appear super sweet. She even gave me a light blue bow to put in my bright red wig. She suggested that I look into using jewels or sparkles around my eyes, and I realized how much potential there was in curating my specific look. We each got dressed and Lil Petal went down the row, fine-tuning us with a few little critiques.

We were now ready to go into town and practice all we had learned. We went to visit a little girl, Kimberly, who had leukemia. She lit up and smiled from ear to ear as we each entered her home. Again, I was inspired to see how much this newfound passion could brighten someone's day, and I craved more.

That evening, Rosemary and I came to the conclusion that since our values and dreams aligned, we should team up; we could do more good together than apart. We started meeting once a week. Rosemary and I ordered the best makeup we could afford, learned how to make balloon animals, and even tried out some sleight of hand magic. We eventually worked out a few routines that helped spread messages of joy and Jesus. Each week, through laughter and playing around, we learned how to be better at our craft, and we knew that the Lord had special plans in store for us.

We started doing small appearances here and there, and we quickly got the attention of our community. People realized pretty fast that we weren't simple circus clowns, and we weren't making any harmful jokes. We were sweet clowns who spread messages of love and joy. One of our first events was the Walla Walla Airshow. We had a blast walking around for hours, laughing and smiling with the community. After that appearance, we were getting invited to gigs left and right, and people started to accept us and our vision; we knew we were on the right path that God was laying out.

One night, Rosemary and I were looking through a catalog of new supplies to order, anything from new costumes to special balloons. As I was flipping through the pages of the catalog, one item stood out to me: a beautiful sticker in the shape of a big red heart that had yellow writing across it saying, *I Hugged A Clown Today*. Something about it made my heart warm, and I put in an order. At our next event, I broke out my new stickers and got a reaction bigger and warmer than I could ever have imagined. Everyone wanted one, and I mean everyone, I went through three hundred to four hundred stickers in about five hours. From angsty teenagers to their middle-aged parents, people stopped mid-stride for a sticker; it was infectious. I had one rule: you had to give a hug before you could get a sticker. These stickers weren't just for show; they were a tool for spreading joy. You could see people with grim faces light up as they got their hug and sticker, and I realized a lot about the people around me, they all craved connection. They all needed that personal touch. The truth is, we never know what anyone is going through. You never know the last time someone was simply hugged. But through the simple power of a sticker, I saw the beginning of a beautiful legacy I could leave. Through the next thirty-five years, I never saw another clown use them. They were my special little trademark.

Everything was falling into place; I had my partner, my mission, and even my trademark sticker, but one thing was still missing: I needed a name.

* * *

It might sound silly, that I went around for so long without a true clown name. I had been consistently clowning for about seven or eight months. The truth is, a name holds so much power, and we rarely get to pick our own. I knew it needed to be special, and I wanted something that would represent me, Cindy, and also my clown persona. I did not know what it would be, but I knew when I heard it, it would click.

One evening, I went to my friend Kathy's house. As I went inside, the sweetest little dog came up to me. His little tail wagged, and he gently licked my nose and ears. Kathy told me all about how she had recently rescued him from a shelter and that he had been abused. You could see in his eyes that he carried some trauma, but you could also see that the love he wanted to give overpowered it. In a moment, I related to this tiny dog; I too had gone through some emotional hurdles growing up, but I was trying to let my love for people overshadow my past hurt. After some sweet cuddles and love, Kathy said, "Sparkle, go lay down," and it was like a lightbulb went off above my head. Sparkle. The name encompassed everything I wanted to show. It was fun, it held hope, it symbolized safety, security, honesty, and compassion. Above all, it symbolized love. All at once, I knew this was the name the Lord had for me.

When things change inside you,
things change around you.

CHAPTER 4

Everyone, Please Welcome Sparkle the Clown!

At this point, I could not have been more confident that I was following the Lord's direction in my life. However, I was not naive to the fact that the people close to me weren't so sure. I am aware that it is a little odd to admit that your mom or wife is a clown, and my family made it clear that they were uncomfortable. My husband at the time had parents who were actively against my new passion. Their cultural superstitions had them believe it was morally and spiritually wrong to be clowning, and they often expressed that they were nervous about what it was doing to my spirit and my children's spirits. My husband also did not approve. He never really understood why I wanted to be Sparkle, and I found myself having to hide this part of my life from him to avoid big fights. I knew he was hoping this was just a passing fad or hobby in my life, one that would go away with a little time. I could tell it embarrassed him to say his wife was a clown, yet he never actively tried to stop me. Other people around me weren't morally against it; they just simply did not understand. All they could picture were circus clowns doing slapstick comedy and embarrassing people; they did not understand the joy and love I was trying to spread.

Despite their disapproval, I wanted to show my family what my clowning was truly about. When an opportunity arose to do just that, I prayed and followed the Lord's direction, way outside of my comfort zone, at my stepsister's wedding. She was getting married at a resort called Silver Saddle in Cal City. It was owned by my youngest sister, Linda, and her husband, Jim. About a week before we left to go to the wedding, I felt convicted that I was supposed to perform "The Rose" at the reception as Sparkle. I knew my husband would strongly disapprove, so I kept my idea a secret and only shared it with Linda. We also knew Jim would not be supportive, so Linda had to keep it from him as well. Whatever reactions our husbands had, we would face them together. She was also apprehensive, nervous about what the family might say and about what negative talk could arise about her venue. There were going to be hundreds of people in attendance at this wedding ready to judge me, and I could tell my sister was trying to save me from that. However, I truly felt like this was what the Lord wanted me to do, and my sister finally agreed to help.

Despite having Linda's approval, I was still nervous. This was not some small appearance I was planning; this was a full-on routine, with music and props in full clown attire in front of my entire family and most of Cal City. I thought this would be a perfect opportunity for my family to finally see what I wanted to do, and that my clowning was different. Maybe they could finally accept me as Sparkle.

As the trip got closer, I continued to keep the plan under wraps. Since we were flying on a small rented plane that my husband was flying, I easily stashed a secret bag with my makeup and costumes in the back of the plane. We arrived Friday afternoon. Almost every minute between then and the ceremony Saturday night, I contemplated backing out, but I held strong. Once we got to the venue, I snuck the bag into one of Linda's back rooms and went to the ceremony as Cindy. After a lovely ceremony, people made their way to the reception for a cocktail hour, and I discreetly snuck away to get ready. As much as I was excited, I was also terrified. I could feel my heart beating outside of my chest. I prayed out loud for the Lord to guide me, give me the words to say, and give the audience accepting hearts. Linda came into my room as I was getting ready and asked me one last time, in a very serious tone, if I was sure that I wanted to do this. Although terrified, I affirmed that I knew this is what the Lord was calling me to do, as crazy as it was. I applied my makeup, got dressed, and made my way to the reception. Linda went to give the sound booth my tape, and I could feel my face get hot – there was no turning back now.

Over the speakers, I heard the MC say, "And now, we have a very special guest here for the bride and groom. Everyone, please welcome… Sparkle the Clown."

I felt everyone's eyes on me all at once. Although I tried not to make eye contact with anyone as I walked out, I saw my husband move towards the back of the room, taking the kids with him. I went straight to the mic and started my speech, wishing the newlyweds good fortune on their new adventure. I started talking about the beauty of a rose, a simple flower some might easily overlook. Yet, it is one of the Lord's greatest gifts to us. Between its beautiful aesthetic and alluring fragrance, it is truly a captivating part of God's creation. I talked about how the rose could symbolize marriage: the petals of a new bud start off tight and close, but when you add the love of the Lord, and love for each other, between the petals, they start to separate and the bud opens up into the most beautiful flower. I kept eye contact with the audience throughout my speech, and it was as if I was reaching each person's soul, so they could feel what I was saying. As I ended my speech, the music began and I looked out into the audience. They were aghast, many with their mouths wide open, but I continued through my routine, hoping it would reach people as it did me when Lil Petal first performed it.

Halfway through, I acted as if I was reaching out to the audience to grab their love and well wishes and put them in a bag to give to the bride and groom. To my surprise, the audience was eager to interact. They reached out and touched my hand, giving me metaphorical love that I neatly placed in the bag. Then, I looked up and reached out to God, grabbing His love and peace and placing those also in the bag. Finally, after everything had been collected, I pulled out the most beautiful rose, smelled it, showed it to the Lord, and then presented it to the bride and groom.

To my amazement, everyone in the room was moved to tears. There was not a dry eye in the house, and I felt acceptance from my family. I could see that they finally understood that my clowning could move people in strong, emotional, and spiritual ways. I found myself crying too.

A few days later, I got to do "The Rose" for my mother and grandmother, who also took the performance to heart and started to see that my clowning was a positive light in my life and in the lives of those around me. The only one who still was not totally on board was my husband. I could see that some little bits were breaking through to him, but I could also tell that he would have preferred if I stopped clowning altogether. Despite seeing the positive reaction I had received in California City, he was still embarrassed by my passion, and he was upset at me for performing at the wedding. Yet I knew the will of the Lord was more important than the embarrassment of my husband, so I continued on.

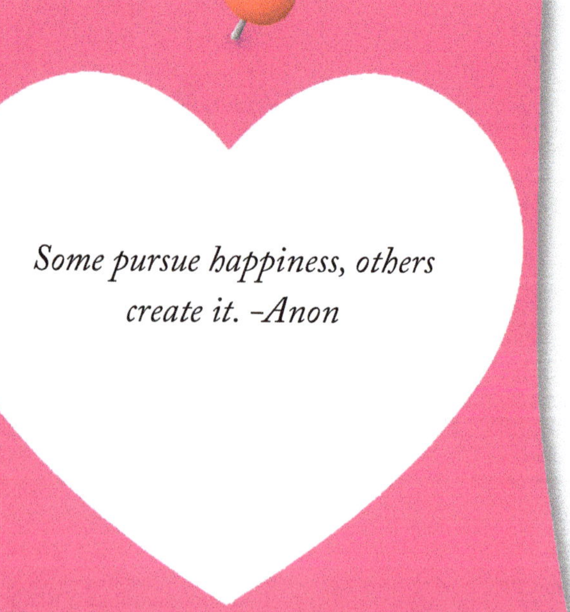
Some pursue happiness, others create it. –Anon

CHAPTER 5

Sparkle's Outfits Over the Years

Rosemary and I had so much fun doing events together, and wherever we were, the people loved us.

We were two totally different types of clowns. I was the sophisticated and proper white-faced clown, and she was the whimsical Auguste Clown named KC (which stood for King's Clown). She wore baggy overalls which went down past her knees, a big striped shirt, tall wild socks, tennis shoes, and a bright lime-green wig with a hat attached. Sometimes she wore gloves with the fingertips cut out.

An Auguste Clown does not have to be completely covered up and can show skin. KC had her face totally brown, with an emphasis on her large eyes, a red nose, soft blush on her cheeks, and a big white smile. Frequently, she would bring her accordion and would play for the kids.

Later, Rosemary made another clown character named Lacey. While KC was more of a tomboy, Lacey was gentle and kind. Lacey was still an Auguste Clown, but she was a softer version, more of a white-faced clown. Lacey wore a soft purple wig with a sweet hat on it. Small, sparkly jewels decorated her cheeks. Rosemary's face was softer as Lacey than KC. She also changed her voice as Lacey. Rosemary loved both of these clowns and showed up to events as whichever one she desired to be that day.

As for Sparkle, I kept my face all white with blush on my cheeks and bright pink and blue eyeshadow. I drew a cute heart on my nose, painted a small happy mouth, and wore long rainbow-colored eyelashes. To pay tribute to my name, I added jewels under my eyes and sparkly glitter all over my face, I truly did sparkle! Rosemary and I always drew the sign of the fish next to our eyes and on our cheeks.

I also came up with my business cards, which made me feel more official. I called myself a special ✝ clown so it sounded like specialty clown, but people knew I was a follower of Christ. I put that at the top of my business cards along with a picture of me, as Sparkle, in a blue and pink jumper with my hands raised, praising God.

I went through a few colors and styles of wigs. There was a time when I wore a metallic silver wig that had hints of color that glistened when I moved. One time I wore a white wig that came down to my shoulders, and I put two royal blue bows on the sides. In my pink wigs, I made beautiful crowns with long ribbons spiraling down through my hair. I put fancy barrettes and different bows and jewels in my wigs. Once I finished with the accessories, I added the final touch, lots of sparkly glitter.

I made the first couple of costumes myself. The first one was a classic, bright red. My second one was made out of a pink flannel one-piece with footies. It was a onesie for kids, and being four foot nine inches at the time, I could fit. I decorated it with royal blue sequins. Then I found a white poofy wig that came down to my shoulders. I decorated the wig by giving it bangs and royal blue bows. It looked really cute. I loved wearing this costume when I knew that I was going to visit the patients at the hospital.

That costume served me well for a while, but at an early point in my clowning, I felt like a metamorphosis was taking place for Sparkle. I needed a new outfit using my favorite color, pink. I used the same jumper pattern that I had used for my red costume, but this time I found pink material and blue material, each with white polka dots. I sewed it so that there was pink on one side and blue on the other. Every clown costume needs pockets, so I added two large ones to carry all of my props. I decorated a pair of white tennis shoes with pink and blue buttons and ribbons. This was my main costume for casual events, but for outings where I needed to be a little fancier, I made another jumper out of bright pink and dazzling blue satin material. I had a wide elastic white belt that I sprayed fine glitter all over. I discovered that satin was not the best clown material to use: even though it was really pretty, it was hot to wear, and inevitably something would spill on it, whether by one of the kids or myself. I found myself always holding my breath until I could get out of it.

I changed my wardrobe only a handful of times over the thirty-five years, at the blessing of three women in my life.

My friend Cara helped me make a really nice costume: it was a beautiful pink pinafore jumper dress. I had a blouse with puffy sleeves and a long, pink, curly wig. She also made a beautiful crown that had fun streamers going down the back and cute little bloomers. I got a pair of white ankle socks and sewed the most adorable buttons on them. I loved this little outfit and wore it for several years.

My next couple of costumes were made by another amazing seamstress, Linda. She made me some of the most beautiful outfits; they were not just fun to wear, but they were also fancy and made me feel like a princess. One was a beautiful pink cotton dress that came to my knees with a sheer apron skirt that tied in the back. My sleeves had three puffs going down my arm to my wrists. I ordered another new long pink curly wig and transferred over my beautiful crown that Cara made me. There were cute hair clips that I found and put in my wig as well. When I was done doing my face and hair, putting the costume on, and sliding on my pink glittery socks and shoes, I was ready, even though it took a long time. I wore this costume for over ten years and I loved it so much.

Near the end of those ten years, it was really looking worn out. I asked my friend Lynn, after I noticed her beautiful seamstress skills, if she would help me make my last costume. We found beautiful silk material that was light and breathable. There were about three different colors of sheer fabric to make different colored aprons. This changed the effect on the dress and made it so I would have three new outfits instead of just one. I could mix and match things since there were also three different collars and two different pink wigs.

I still feel so blessed by those three women who helped me bring the magic of Sparkle to life. When my beautiful friends were not helping me with outfits, the Lord was at work picking out his own special touches, including the perfect shoes!

One of my favorite times of year was Halloween. I would scour stores for new makeup and accessories for Sparkle. I always wiped stores clean of their eye jewelry or rainbow eyelashes. It was fun to walk the aisles to see what else I could add to my costume. During one of my trips to the local Halloween store, I felt an overwhelming sense that the Lord had something special for me to find in the store that day. Nothing was calling out to me, but I still had a gut feeling to keep looking. It was near the end of October; the store was in complete disarray. Boxes were misplaced and turned over, and costumes were in a hodgepodge of sizes and colors.

I felt the Lord calling me to the shoe area, one of the most jumbled. There were shoes scattered everywhere in different piles, and it was hard to even find a matching pair, let alone something one was actually looking for. Yet I could not shake the feeling that the Lord wanted me to look through the pile, so I did. I knew it would be difficult to find anything I would actually want; it is pretty hard to find shoes that fit me in the first place since I am a tiny, and rare, size five. The first box I picked up were some of the ugliest shoes that I had ever seen, and I quickly put them back. Then I picked up a second box from the ground, not knowing what color, style, or even size was inside. To my amazement, I saw the most beautiful, sparkly pink shoes. They reminded me of Dorothy's shoes from the *Wizard of Oz*, but instead of red, they were pink, Sparkle's signature color. Not only that, but they were discounted and in my size! I was so excited I could barely stand it.

I took the shoes to the register, beaming from ear to ear and raving about the shoes to the cashier who was visibly confused. She said, "Where did you get these? I haven't seen any shoes like this before; I had no idea we sold them." I knew it was not a coincidence. It was God putting his finishing touch on Sparkle's outfit. I went on to wear those beautiful shoes for the next fifteen years.

Keep your face always toward the sunshine and shadows will fall behind you! –Walt Whitman

CHAPTER 6

Parades and Purpose

As the years went by, Rosemary and I attended as many community events as we could. The Chamber of Commerce started hiring us for almost every fair or festival that came around, and soon we were visiting fall festivals, air shows, hospitals, parades, and more. We were both having a great time and especially enjoyed it when we got together weekly to work out more gospel-centered routines, learn new magic tricks, and practice new balloon animals.

One of my favorite events was the yearly Blooming Onion Festival. There was one booth, owned by a local family, that had the best flavored onions you can imagine. They got their onions from a local farmer and made sauces to go on the onions. Never in my life did I think I would want to eat an entire onion like an apple, but every year I looked forward to their onions sprinkled with their special spices. It was my special treat after a long day.

Every year, with the exception of only one or two, I participated in the Walla Walla Fair and Frontier Days Parade. Originally, I was one of the only clowns there. Year after year, more clowns participated, and eventually the commission even created a clown category to judge us on appearance, attitudes, and crowd participation. Although I was proud to take home the blue ribbon for my category almost every year, it was still the smiles and connection with people that made me the most happy.

For the vast majority of the parades, I did not even make it to the finish line; I was too busy running back and forth in a zigzag from either side of the parade trying to give out as many hugs as I could. It seemed that there was never enough time. It was impossible for me to ignore a child calling out to me by name. I was so behind that eventually they put me in the front of the parade so I could set the pace, and when even that turned out to be difficult, I rode in a horse and buggy the last few years, waving to everyone.

As much fun as these events were, they were also pretty time-consuming. It took me nearly two hours to get ready for each event. Once I got home, it would take me an hour to get the makeup off and another hour in the shower scrubbing down. It seemed silly to go through four hours of getting ready and cleaning up to only clown for two hours, so it was common for me to continue clowning after events were over. I would often stop in hospitals, nursing homes, or our Christian Aid Center to see what kind of joy I could continue to spread.

People regularly pointed out to me that I could cut my getting-ready time in half if I stopped worrying about being so detailed and consistent, but that was not an option in my mind. Imagine going to Disney World and seeing Cinderella only halfway done with makeup; it would ruin the magic, and it would be obvious to kids that she was a different person each time. I wanted to look the exact same way every time, so that kids who met me previously knew exactly who I was the next time they saw me. I wanted kids who had seen me as they were growing up to recognize me when they were teenagers and adults. Also, the effort to get ready seemed minimal compared to the joy I was spreading. On the days it was hot, I would still go out in a full dress, wig, gloves, and pantyhose, because by the end of the day, I would give out three to four hundred hugs, and those hugs meant more to me than any inconvenience. Keeping this magic alive was just as important to me as keeping my integrity as Sparkle whenever I was in any sort of public setting. I took it very seriously that kids recognized me and knew who I was whenever I was out of the house. I was reminded of just how important my integrity as Sparkle was one year at the Balloon Stampede. KC and I attended the event like normal, going around doing sleight of hand magic, making balloon animals, and giving out hugs. Also in attendance was a Ronald McDonald clown who was putting on a show for the children. However, when the children realized we were there, they started leaving his show to come visit us. We were asked by his security to leave the area and tell the children to go back to Ronald McDonald; he was clearly irritated with our presence, but we obliged. After the show was over, I turned a corner to find him, still in full costume, smoking a cigarette. I was utterly disgusted, not so much at the smoking, but at the fact that he was willing to do it so publicly with children still walking around. I always committed to being Sparkle, no matter how long, if I was in potential eyesight of the public. The ethics of it all were, and are still, so important to me.

When one door of happiness closes, another opens; but often we look so long at the closed door that we do not see the one which has been opened for us.
–Helen Keller

CHAPTER 7

Princesses and Heroes

When I started doing birthday parties, kids had the best time, and I did too. Word spread about how much fun my parties were, and it seemed that I was always booked. They were about an hour to an hour and a half long, but I still spent a lot of time preparing my tricks for the parties and getting dressed up.

There was a typical flow to birthday parties. When I first got there, I set my things down, got all of the kids around me, and we played games together. The games were usually *Hot Ball*, *Red Light*, *Green Light*, and *Tossing Balls into a Glass Jar*. After a couple of games, the children were engaged and eager to participate.

Gathering all of the kids, I had them sit down around me. Then I spoke directly to the birthday child. If it was a girl, I let everyone know that she was a princess for the day. I put a sparkling crown on her head, a fluffy pink boa around her neck, and I gave her a wand to use. If the birthday child was a boy, I told everyone that he was a star or hero, like Superman. I even had a flowing red cape that I put on the birthday boy. He too got to use one of my wands.

Once our birthday child was grinning and in their celebratory costume, I called up several different kids to help me with sleight of hand magic tricks. Along with the sleight of hand, I also did a few magic tricks with messages on hope, healing, and love. Many parents stood around to watch these performances, and I was grateful to have the chance to not only impact the kids but other adults as well.

Balloon animals were always a favorite with the kids (and even a lot of the adults). All of the children got a balloon animal to play with and take home.

After everyone got a balloon animal, I told a story that had a lot of positive morals for the kids to think about. I frequently read, *The Whistling Frog from Lily Pad Pond*, by William Crain. There is a quote on the front of the book that I think sums it up perfectly: "If you don't even try, you will never know, how great you can be, and how far you can go".

Near the end, I opened the floor to questions in case the kids had any. Then I would pull out my kazoo and play "Happy Birthday,"and everyone would jump in to sing. Usually I was very out of tune, but it still was fun and made people laugh.

Finally, I gave the birthday child a present from Sparkle. Then I gave everyone a hug and handed out my *I Hugged A Clown Today!* stickers. These birthday parties not only created sweet memories for me, but I met teenagers or adults years later who remembered the special birthday I gave them as a child.

I had *Free Hug Coupons* that I gave to the adults before I left that said, "Good for one hug. Redeemable from any participating human being." My friend Bill started the hug coupons, and we were close because he was like a brother to me growing up. I asked if I could use his idea and make it my own for Sparkle, and he agreed. I gave out thousands of these cards over the years, but I know Bill gave out double or triple what I did. Those were his special gift to bless people that he met in his life. I would give a card to a husband and another to his wife, so they could pass them back and forth to each other. At other places I would leave them out for waitresses after my tip, or find strangers to share them with. They were a special way I could brighten someone's day even after I had left.

* * *

Doing the birthday parties was a lot of fun and word spread quickly. It seemed that I was always busy, but there was a hefty cost that my kids and I paid.

I had my day job, where I worked forty hours a week. My family was so important to me, and I tried to balance my time with them too. My two beautiful kids sacrificed a lot to let me pursue this wonderful calling placed on my life.

I knew that the Lord was calling me to be Sparkle through those years, but it was also very challenging. When I was working activities like parades, fairs, or community events, I could not spend that time walking around with my kids. I also stayed in character the whole time, to keep the magic of Sparkle alive to anyone who saw her. I have memories of my children when they were young running up to me calling, "Mom! Mom!"

I would bend down and whisper, "I'm not Mom, I'm Sparkle." This would break my heart, telling them not to call me mom. As they grew up though, I could see that they were proud of me and understood the impact that Sparkle had and the unique calling on my life from the Lord.

Now I would like to specifically acknowledge my son, David, and my daughter, Jennifer. They were then, and still are, the most wonderful kids that I could have ever asked for.

I want to thank both of you for loving me so much and allowing me to be Sparkle the Clown. I knew as you were growing up, especially as a teenager, it was hard saying to other kids, "My mom is a clown." Yet you always showed up to any events that I did, right up until I retired.

Thank you, from the bottom of my heart.

Happiness is a by-product of helping others. -Denny Miller

CHAPTER 8

Sparkle's Special Children

During those years, we met thousands of people, and I handed out thousands of stickers and hugs. Yet there were a few people I met who will always hold a special place in my heart, including one little girl named Heather.

Heather was a very beautiful four-year-old girl who was physically challenged and had a lot of health issues that made most tasks, including simply walking, very difficult. I met her at one event, and she soon fell in love with me. Her parents asked me to come to her fifth birthday party where KC and I pulled out all the stops. We played games, did magic, made balloon animals, told stories, and even presented her with a very special birthday gift. In actuality, Heather blessed me more than anything I could have ever given her. Throughout the years of knowing her, I watched as she committed herself to ballet. Although she struggled a bit on stage, her smile was infectious and she inspired me to continue to spread joy.

During these years, I also met two beautiful children named Tonya and Brian. I had heard through the local news that there were two little toddlers that now lived in Walla Walla after a tragic drowning accident where they both nearly died and were left with debilitating physical and mental damage. Both kids were totally paralyzed, relied on feeding tubes, and could only communicate with little grunts, squirms, or blinks. After hearing their story, I knew I had to at least try to meet them and lift their spirits, even if only for an afternoon.

I was a little nervous; it is not every day a clown shows up to your door, and I did not know how the parents would react or if they would even welcome me in. When I got to their house, I explained my desire to meet the children, and the parents were excited. They warned me that it could be emotionally triggering to see two children in this state, but I braced myself and just tried to think positively.

As much as I had tried to prepare myself, it was a pretty upsetting sight. The two children were hooked up to a plethora of monitors, and the family room looked like a hospital. The children could not move much at all, but I could see their eyes light up when I walked in. I went over to them, trying to keep a smile on my face, and focused on them. I sat and talked, rubbed their arms, and tried to keep eye contact. I could tell they were relaxing a bit. I broke out a few magic tricks and balloon animals and told them a few stories. Although it was incredibly sad to witness, I also felt honored to be with them and give them some joy. After almost every event I attended as Sparkle, I would stop by their house to check on them. Each time their little eyes, filled with joy, made mine tear up. I was honored to have known them, and was thankful for my time with them when they passed away.

A few years later, their parents had another child named Grace, whom I got to watch grow up and go to college. She was a beautiful child who often reminded me of her siblings and the cherished time I had with them. It was families like these, with wonderful children that I kept meeting, that reminded me I was doing God's will.

While I often felt as if I was doing the Lord's work, there were many times where I got to see Him work while I was Sparkle. One time in particular stands out to me about a little girl named Kimberly. As you might remember, Kimberly was a young girl I had met in my early days as a clown, before I even had a name. She was a sweet five-year-old who suffered from leukemia. Throughout my years as Sparkle, Rosemary and I, and sometimes Rosemary's daughter, Molly, would go visit Kimberly to check in on her. We grew very close over the years, and it warmed my heart to always hear her refer to us as her clowns.

One day, Rosemary got the call that Kimberly had taken a hard turn for the worse in her health. She had a bad infection that the doctors could not cure, and her white blood cell count was too low to fight it off. Kimberly was quickly dying and was given just a few days, or maybe even hours, left to live.

We were told that Kimberly, in her pain, was calling out to her clowns for comfort. Since she was staying at the Ronald McDonald House in Seattle, the workers there assumed she was asking for the Shriners clowns. When they arrived, Kimberly only cried more and insisted she wanted her clowns.

As soon as we heard this, we knew we had to get to her, and quickly. The community around us banded together and almost instantly got us money to pay for our bus tickets. Local companies also donated bags of toys to bring to Kimberly and the other children, which we loaded onto the bus in the middle of the night.

Rosemary and I prayed that entire trip that we would make it in time to see Kimberly. We also prayed over her condition and asked God to guide us in how to handle this precious and delicate time with her. We had already seen how He could bring the community together to help us get to her, so we knew His hand, like always, was with us.

After eight hours, we got off at our destination. Kimberly's dad met us there. He took us to a nearby grocery store where we tried as fast as we could to get into our clown attire and makeup. All of this was kept a surprise to Kimberly, and we were eager to get to her.

As soon as we went into her room, her face lit up, as if she was not sick at all. "My clowns! My clowns!" she screamed with excitement. Although it was hard to see her in her most fragile state, it was heartwarming to see how the Lord was using us to help her. We sat and opened some presents with her before telling her that we had another big surprise in store.

Her mom wheeled her down to the main room, where many other patients were excitedly waiting. Kimberly sat right in the middle as we put on a show for all the kids. She was our main star, our princess. Kimberly giggled, squealed, and wiggled with excitement the rest of the day; anyone who looked on the scene would never have guessed how sick she truly was.

The idea of leaving her for the last time was so difficult that Rosemary and I decided to stay until the very last second, causing us to board our bus back home still fully dressed as KC and Sparkle. While it amused the passengers, and I tried to be my most Sparkle self for them, it was extremely hard knowing what Kimberly was facing.

Two days later we got a call from Kimberly's mom, Jodi. We braced ourselves for what we thought was the inevitable news as we picked up the phone, but to our amazement, Jodi's voice was cheery. "You will never believe this," she started, "but after you guys left on Saturday, Kimberly's white blood cells shot up in a way the doctors can't explain. The infection is gone, and she is coming home tomorrow." We sat together, bawling, in awe of the miracle God had let us witness and be a part of.

Sometimes I just look up, smile and say, "I know that was you. Thank you."

CHAPTER 9

Signs and Wonders at the Fairground

Some days that I spent clowning would be predictable; I knew what my day would look like if I was attending a birthday party, or even visiting children at the local hospital. However, there were a few times I left the house as Sparkle where I had no idea what the Lord had in store for me and that I would come back home changed for the better. One of those days was when I left to attend the annual Balloon Stampede.

I was doing the event as normal, entertaining families with magic and stories and handing out a lot of hugs, when I noticed one family with three young children off to the side. They kept watching me, but never came close. When the crowd around me started to dissipate, I went up to the family to introduce myself. I started with the oldest child, Anna, but the mom quickly cut me off saying, "Anna is deaf and can't hear you, so don't worry about trying to talk to her."

Rather than ignore her, I got excited. I knew a little American Sign Language (ASL) and was happy to finally use it. I faced Anna and signed, "Hello. You are so beautiful! I am glad to meet you."

Her face lit up instantly, as if this was the first time in a long time that she could talk to someone. Her hands moved quickly, and I could tell she was ecstatic to communicate. I did not know enough to understand, but her parents interpreted for me. We sat there for a few minutes, signing back and forth, and when I looked up, her parents had tears in their eyes. It was clear Anna did not get to interact with others that often and that this would be something she and I would remember for a long time. I turned around to see a camera crew starting to film our interaction. I wanted this to be a pure moment for her, not a spectacle for others. I wanted her to feel normal and loved. So I gave them their hugs and stickers and walked off in the opposite direction of the cameras. As I walked, I thought about how important that moment was and how imperative it is that everyone feel loved, no matter their disabilities or differences. Right then I decided I would enroll at the local college and take a few ASL classes.

I was so excited about my time with Anna, but I was also very tired. I had been at the Balloon Stampede for about five hours, and I was ready to go home. It was never as easy as simply walking out of the exit, considering I never turned down anyone who called out to me. As I got close to leaving, I saw large crowds of people ahead of me split like the Red Sea. They were clearly uncomfortable and trying to get away from the gang that was making their way inside of the festival.

The gang was dressed in black with a tough glint in their eyes and tight lips. It was clear who their leader was, especially when we locked eyes. He was extremely tall, dressed in all black from head to toe with a large leather trench coat over top. He had piercings and tattoos covering almost every inch of his hands and face. He had thick chains clanking against his legs as he walked straight towards me. Even though I knew in my heart that the Lord had always protected me, I could not help but be scared, and I gripped my skunk puppet a little tighter.

He came straight up to me, towering almost two feet over me as his group created a circle around us. I looked up and locked eyes with him, trying to be brave.

"So what have you got there?" he said somewhat smugly, pointing to my bag.

"I have my *I Hugged A Clown Today!* stickers," I said back, trying to stay in character.

"Well, ya going to give me one or what?" he said.

"I mean, not without a hug first," I said.

I almost could not believe it. Here I was, all four feet and nine inches of me, surrounded by gang members, telling their leader that he could not have a sticker unless he hugged me. He stared at me for about twenty seconds, which felt like an eternity, while I contemplated whether I had made the right move or not.

"Well, okay," he said, somewhat quietly. Suddenly, his huge body started to lower. I reached up as he put his arms under mine, and we stayed there for a moment, embracing. It felt like no one else was around. His whole body seemed to let go of some of the tension that it had been holding onto for who knows how long, and he just melted into me. It was honestly one of the best hugs I have ever received.

It was only a short time, but it made me rethink so much about what I thought I knew. So many questions flooded my mind: when was the last time this young man hugged someone? When was the last time he felt wanted or loved? When was the last time this young man had any sort of encounter with someone who knew Jesus?

He eventually broke free, and the group around us started to follow him as he walked away. "Wait. You forgot your sticker." I yelled.

He looked back at me, differently this time; there was a new light in his eyes and he walked a little lighter. He came towards me again and I peeled off a bright red sticker and stuck it straight onto his black trenchcoat. "Thank you," he said as he smiled down at me.

"No, thank you." I beamed back.

I don't know his name, or whether he even remembers that moment, but all these years later I can tell you for certain that in that moment, God taught me such an important lesson: everyone, no matter their circumstance or where they come from, is a child of God. Everyone deserves to be loved. Everyone deserves to be hugged.

From then on, whenever I encountered gangs or people who might be different from me, I remembered the man in the black trenchcoat and the lesson he taught me. He helped me see people as God sees people: lost and in need of love.

Anytime you doubt yourself, remember, you are a strong soul who shines after any storm. You can literally get through anything. You have demonstrated that time and time again. Keep going! Keep shining! You got this! –Kristen Butler

CHAPTER 10

A Graduation to Remember

In a moment of honesty, I want to pause my stories here for a second to share with you that the journey to complete this book has not been easy. I have had constant doubts of whether writing this book is something that God is really calling me to do, and whether now is even the best time to do it. Yet I have found that when I simply ask God for a sign, He gives me an answer. This week He gave me my answer, but it starts with a story about a preschool graduation that took place almost fifteen years ago.

Noah's Ark was the name of a large daycare facility in Walla Walla that was known for loving children and never turning one away. One year, they asked for Sparkle to perform at their preschool graduation, which I was so excited to do. Not only did I obviously love performing for children, but I used this event as an opportunity to invite my good friend, Lew, to come watch. Lew was someone I had met at my day job, and he was pretty skeptical about my clowning. Similar to my family, he had only ever thought of clowns as white-faced weirdos doing slapstick comedy, and I was excited to show him the softer side of clowning.

To my surprise, Lew came to the graduation and sat directly in the middle of the third row to have a good view. He was amazed at the reaction kids and adults had when I walked in the room. Everyone knew me and everyone wanted to be around me. They were there not because of some silly tricks that I did, but because of what Sparkle had grown to mean to the community: kindness, integrity, understanding, and above all, love.

When I got up on stage, I did my introduction in American Sign Language (ASL) and then performed a skit to Barbra Streisand's "I Believe" and "When You Walk Through a Storm." Everyone in the room was teary-eyed by the end of it, including Lew, who later admitted he had not cried in years. I had been divorced for a little while, so Lew's friendship and support meant a lot to me. Little did we know that in a few years, we would be shedding tears at our own wedding.

I had not thought about that preschool graduation in many years, but as I mentioned, God used that memory to give me comfort this week. A few days ago, I was at the hospital for an appointment of mine. Obviously I was not dressed up as Sparkle, but to my amazement, as I was talking to a security guard, one of his female colleagues came running up to me asking if I was Sparkle the Clown. I looked at her slightly surprised, but said, "Yes. I am."

She seemed teary-eyed, but excited, as she told me that she had watched a tape the previous night of her son's preschool graduation at Noah's Ark. She had not watched it since the event, but she said as she watched it, her heart was so warmed at how I had cared for the children of the preschool that day, including her son, Isaiah. She told me that he had sadly passed away a few years ago, and the night before she was searching for a happy memory of him, so she watched the tape. Little did she know that at the same time she was watching that tape, I was praying to God to give me a sign of affirmation that my time as Sparkle was important, and that putting those stories down in a book was something He wanted me to do. She told me that it was her last day working there at the hospital. I was so thankful to run into her and was amazed by how good God's timing is.

Hope is the pillar that holds up the world. Hope is the dream of a waking man. –Pliny, the Elder

CHAPTER 11

Happy Birthday Jesus

One day in late autumn my friend and I were in the car listening to the radio when a song came on that I'll never forget. We were headed to Tri-Cities to go Christmas shopping when the song, "Happy Birthday Jesus," began to play. I was immediately struck by the gentle melody and captivating lyrics. Once I heard that song, I did everything I could to hear it again. This was about twenty to thirty years ago, when the internet was not as good of a resource as it is now. I went into Christian bookstores to inquire about this song until finally I found it: "Happy Birthday Jesus" by the Brooklyn Tabernacle Choir. I still have the original CD that I bought in the store that day.

I had already fallen in love with the song, and I knew the Lord wanted me to do something special with it. First, I incorporated the little sign language I knew to go along with the song. Then I practiced a routine with expressions and movements to bring the song to life even more. I prayed to ask the Lord what I should do with this beautiful song. After weeks of waiting and prayer, it finally came to me! I knew it would take a miracle for this to happen, but God is the God of miracles.

I could picture the whole routine for a lovely Christmas play. The idea was to blend the song "Happy Birthday Jesus" with the art of theatre to create a live visual celebration of the beautiful birth of Jesus. It was so clear and strong in my heart that I could not shake it. I knew it was the Lord's will and He would bless this idea that He had given me.

Now I needed my pastor to be on board. I attended a conservative church, and many of the people there were traditional and did not like change in the service.

My pastor, Pastor Thomas, was from another country and more of a theologian, so it took some convincing on my end. I played the song for him. While he was interested, he was concerned about how the congregation would react, having a clown perform on stage during the service. However, he finally agreed and the door was opened for this new project, as long as we did it before the actual service started. He was putting a lot of trust in this program as he had no idea what to expect because he had never seen anything like this before.

With Pastor Thomas' approval, I was able to pursue this dream.

The following Sabbath, I went to each of the Sabbath School classes to share my idea and invite children to participate in this program. I told everyone I was Sparkle the Clown, and we would create a beautiful play to honor the birth of Jesus. Many children were interested and excited to participate in this play. We started rehearsing, and the drama club at church let us borrow costumes. Someone donated Christmas trees for us to use, which was such a blessing to our performance.

At our first rehearsal, I met one of the most incredible ladies ever. Her name was Peggy, and she watched while her daughters rehearsed as the carolers. Peggy noticed that I was trying to incorporate sign language into the performance, and she offered to help me. I eagerly agreed, and we worked closely on the performance after that. This was the start of a beautiful friendship.

Growing up, my mother was hard of hearing, so there was a lot of lip reading and an introduction to sign language in my home. I knew how critical it was to create an inclusive environment, so being able to learn and express my work through sign language was important to me.

Peggy and I started meeting during the week to plan the performance, but we quickly grew a beautiful friendship. Peggy even shared that she desired to be a clown too, and to make a difference with her life. We sometimes clowned together and I shared tips with her. We went to a few places to perform like hospitals and festivals and had a great time sharing joy with others.

We worked hard on the routine for many weeks, until it was finally time for the performance. The play was only the length of the song, but we wanted to make sure each moment was purposeful and brought to life the story of Jesus' birth.

A couple of weeks before Christmas, we were ready. The kids were full of jittery excitement on the day of our play. I was excited too, but I was also nervous because the congregation was mostly elderly people who looked at clowning differently than I did. It was going to be an eye-opener for the majority of the people there. I was nervous too because Pastor Thomas had put his trust in me and I did not want the congregation to be mad at him.

The play was about to start.

People gasped in excitement and surprise when the kids walked out on stage, dressed in costumes of carolers, shepherds, Mary and Joseph. Right when the song began to play, I walked out as Sparkle.

Happy birthday Jesus.

I walked out onto the stage, miming the lyrics.

I'm so glad it's Christmas.

I turned toward the beautiful, sparkling tree on the stage.

All the tinsel and lights.

I picked up a big wrapped present from under the tree.

And the presents are nice.

I walked over to where Mary and Joseph stood over baby Jesus.

But the real gift is you.

There was a pause and then the stage burst to life as the kids jumped in with singing and bells and the love of Jesus bursting forth.

The play continued with joy as we sang, mimed, and signed the song. At the end were the beautiful lyrics:

Happy birthday, Jesus

Jesus I love you

I love you Jesus.

I knelt down in respect by Jesus' cradle as the song ended.

The congregation burst into applause with people rejoicing and calling out "Amen!" The children had done a fantastic job. Everyone found great joy in our performance that we had given to the Lord. Pastor Thomas was delighted that he had said yes to this opportunity, and that most people had accepted me as Sparkle. The performance was impactful for me, the kids, and the congregation. Even years later, people would tell me how impactful the play was to them and their children. There was one gentleman who would talk about the play for years, even as his daughter, who played Mary, was into her twenties.

The Lord brought forth this beautiful gift out of nothing, out of two friends going shopping and listening to Christmas carols on the radio. By listening to the Lord's calling on my heart, I was able to be a part of a special gift to the families in our church.

Hope arouses, as nothing else can arouse, a passion for the possible.
–William Sloan Coffin, Jr.

CHAPTER 12

The Rehab Center

No visitors were allowed in the locked-up ward for addicts.

That is what rehab centers were called in the 1990s. Locked wards had bars on the windows and kept their doors bolted shut. Patients were not allowed any contact with family or friends until their recovery was complete. While there could be healing and restoration for people struggling with addiction, it could also be a lonely and scary place.

The word was spreading about what the Lord was doing through Sparkle. I was being asked to visit abused or terminally ill children, nursing homes, schools, and a variety of places that needed a spark of hope.

One day I was asked if I would be willing to visit patients in a locked ward where they helped the people struggling with addiction. They wanted to see if this would help some of the patients open up and talk. I was a little scared because some people in the locked ward were going through withdrawals and were angry that they were in there. Yet this was another avenue to reach the hurting. So of course I said yes! I was doing this for the Lord, and I needed to be present. I went from room to room visiting with the patients. For some of them, that was the first time they had smiled in a very long time.

I showed all of the people love and kindness, along with encouragement on their recovery. Through my childhood and adult life, I experienced extended stays in hospitals and recovery units. As a child, I had many physical conditions to overcome. I was born with cerebral palsy and was numb from the waist down. My recovery was incredibly long, and I remember wearing braces on both of my legs in second grade and falling frequently. The Lord blessed me and helped me overcome many of the symptoms that accompanied that disorder, but in eighth grade I was in a horse-riding accident. I was paralyzed and in a coma for nineteen days. The doctors said I would never recover from this accident, yet miraculously I did. As an adult, I suffered from an eating disorder that required time spent at a recovery unit. Through all of those experiences, I understood what it was like to feel deep physical pain and fall into despair. I also understood the importance of hope. Through my experiences, others were able to not only relate but see that hope and love are a real possibility for their future as well.

One of my favorite tricks as a clown was the sleight of hand with the pink heart.

I would hold up a full, crisp pink heart and say, "What is this?"

They would say that it was a heart and I would respond, "It's not just any heart, it symbolizes our heart." Then I would continue, "There are things every day that happen to us. Some days your heart feels this big."

I would hold up the whole, full heart.

"Then there are other days that it doesn't work out. Maybe you are getting a divorce." I would rip the heart and continue tearing it into smaller pieces as I gave more examples.

"Maybe you are struggling at work, or you've lost a loved one. Maybe recovery has been more difficult than you anticipated."

At this point, I had shredded scraps of paper in my hands.

"When you've been impacted by someone who really loves you, then you are allowing the Lord to come inside of you." I would hold out my cupped hands and tell them to touch my hands. I reminded them of the torn heart, and then I opened my hands to reveal a whole heart. There were no scraps, no torn paper. Only a complete heart.

"When the Lord is inside you, then you can be made whole."

It meant a lot to the patients and staff that Sparkle was there. The staff noted that Sparkle's presence brought encouragement and hope to their healing process. After my first visit with the people in recovery, I was told that I could go back and visit the patients whenever I wanted. For a long time afterwards, I would visit the people in recovery and spend time with them.

I was amazed by all of the doors that the Lord was opening through Sparkle, and I felt blessed that He was allowing me to be a part of His plan. As long as Jesus was in control of this crazy tandem bike ride, I would continue to sit on the back seat, hold on tight, and peddle as fast as I could! I knew that it was going to be an exciting, meaning ful, and very touching ride.

I am with you always (remaining with you perpetually–regardless of circumstance, and on every occasion), even to the end of the age. –Matthew 28:20

CHAPTER 13

Clown Communion

When KC and I were still clowning together, we were asked by a neighboring church if we could put on a show for the youth group at their gathering. It would be the week before Easter. We eagerly agreed. After much thought and prayer, we decided to ask the pastor if he would let us do a clown communion. We told him our plan, and he agreed.

Clown communion was something I learned when I first started clowning. KC took me to a clowning class that taught different techniques and skills for clowning. Our teacher, Lil Petal, taught us clown communion. KC and I were going to expand on what she taught us to make it even more impactful.

We prepared the stage before it was time to perform. Where the pastor would normally stand, we placed a large hot pink tote box. Inside the tote were all of our props.

KC and I stayed out of sight as the kids filed in and took their seats. They stared curiously at the pink tote which sat on an empty table. Soft music began to play, and the room became quiet. The room would stay draped in a voiceless silence the rest of the performance as our whole show was mimed.

KC and I walked down the middle aisle towards the tote. We looked curiously at this beautiful plastic box, walking around it as if inspecting it. Placed on top was a large note. We picked it up to read it, appearing shocked by what it said. Then we turned the note to face the crowd.

TO: YOU
WITH LOVE: GOD

We looked quizzically upward, as if asking God if this was really for us. We appeared to hear God's "Yes." We smiled at each other and then began to take items one at a time out of the box.

First, we pulled out a wicker basket. Appearing unsure what to do with the basket, we placed it to the side and pulled out the next item. It was a simple wooden cross. Again we looked heavenward, seeming to ask what to do with the cross. It was as if the Lord said, "Trust me." We gently set the cross down.

Then we gingerly reached inside and pulled out sharp wires and barbs. It was a metal crown of thorns. We shared a confused look, but trusted in God's plan. We placed it tenderly on the head of the cross.

Next we pulled out a plain, beige goblet. At this point, KC and I acted convinced that we had no idea what was occurring. We looked around at all the items, trying to puzzle together what they had in common and how they could relate to each other. We placed the goblet on the table next to the cross.

KC peered into the bag for the next item and looked up at me with a wide smile and delight in her eyes. She waved me over to look inside with her. I looked inside as she reached down and lovingly pulled out a long, soft loaf of bread. It was wrapped snugly in white linen, as if it was a swaddled baby. KC handed the loaf to me and I rocked it gently, looking as if I was whispering and cooing to a baby. Then I showed the loaf to the audience, as if letting my closest friends meet my baby for the first time. I tucked the loaf safely into the cozy wicker basket.

Without warning, KC and I looked up sharply, as if the great voice of God had just spoken. We shook our heads with wild and fearful eyes, daring to try and deny the voice of God. We could not do what He was asking.

Yet the great voice of God seemed to overwhelm us, not only with power, but with a desire for us to surrender and trust Him.

We lowered our heads in submission, nodding in despairing agreement. I looked at what I was holding, this beautiful symbolic baby that I had just shown so lovingly to my friends only a few moments ago. I turned to look at all of the other gifts we had taken out of the box. We went up to the cross, and KC gently lifted our loved loaf from the basket. I tenderly removed the swaddle, unraveling the carefully placed white linen.

Real tears stung my eyes as I lifted the bare loaf to heaven. I brought the loaf to my chest. I met KC's eyes, which were rimmed with real, heartfelt tears.

Then I ripped the loaf in half.

Everyone gasped, staring in silent shock at what we had done. KC lifted the goblet off of the table and raised it to heaven, another offering to God. I too raised the bread, letting the Lord bless these items.

KC turned to me, and I ripped off a smaller piece of bread, dipping it into the goblet. The bread came out stained red, causing the youth to marvel again. I ate the bread in dipped juice, and KC did the same.

We set everything on the table, and then humbly bowed our heads in gratitude to the Lord. Our presentation was over.

The pastor came forward then, blessing the bread and juice for communion.

This presentation was incredibly impactful for me, KC, the pastor, and the youth. Communion is the holy sacrament that remembers and honors the night before Christ died on the cross. The breaking of the bread and drinking of the juice reminds us of the great sacrifice Christ made when his body was broken and his blood shed. This holy moment can become habitual for some, but that night the reality of Christ's sacrifice came to life in the symbolic presentation of the bread as an innocent baby, just as Christ died a pure and innocent man. To show the youth this powerful reminder of communion was a gift KC and I were grateful to share with them.

Most folks are about as happy
as they make up their minds to be.
– Abraham Lincoln

CHAPTER 14

Woodstick

Mike Hammond was the type of person who could cast a vision that would impact the whole community, and he did.

Mike was a hippie who stepped straight out of the sixties and had not looked back. He was older than me and kept his long hair tied in a ponytail down his back. Mike had a great passion for music. He owns Melody Muffler, a car shop in Walla Walla.

Mike owned several acres of land that sat near the top of a mountain, with a long winding road and rich green vegetation marking the way. In 1992, Mike began to dream of a space where people could come together through the love of fellowship and music. Mike was a fantastic musician, and he loved to share the joy of music with others. He cleared trees and brush to open up a large grassy field on his property. Mike called his event Woodstick as a nod to the free-spirited and music-loving event, Woodstock.

In the early summer of 1993, Woodstick held its first event.

It was a disaster.

Mike's property was trashed as droves of people came to reenact the drug-induced, alcohol stupor from the original Woodstock days. Many came dressed as hippies, and revisited old hippie habits as well. His property was left uncared for and unappreciated. This was devastating to Mike, who had imagined a day of true, lighthearted merriment and familial fun.

The second year resulted similarly to the first, which is why when it was time for the third annual Woodstick event, Mike had a plan, and part of that plan was me.

Mike invited me to come to Woodstick to help promote a family-friendly environment. Alcohol and drugs were banned. The admission fee was two dollars and a can of food for their food bank. The fee and extra donations went to providing instruments for kids in schools who could not afford it. The event was on track to be just like Mike imagined.

The day of the event, I was a little nervous. It was a pleasant Saturday morning at the beginning of summer. The event started at 10:00 a.m. and ran through the evening. Mike put forth a lot of effort into making the event family-focused, and I was a critical part of that. Sparkle was listed as a special guest on posters all around the city.

I parked and walked towards the entrance, already in full swing as Sparkle. As I reached the front gate, I saw several tall, muscular men with long wild hair wearing thick boots, black leather jackets, and dark sunglasses. They looked like a motorcycle gang that rode around with Hell's Angels. I smiled in relief. They were Mike's friends.

They smiled and waved when they saw me approaching. One of them lifted me into a huge hug, my feet clear off of the grass. They were working security for Mike, checking bags and ensuring a safe environment. They even reassured me that they would keep an eye on me to make sure I was safe. No one ever harmed me as Sparkle, but I could not help but feel my racing heart calm at their promise.

They were a rough-looking group, but their hearts were the sweetest. As the morning progressed, families trickled in with kids, picnic baskets, dogs, and laughter. The canned food pile grew huge, and an old-fashioned glass water cooler was repurposed as a donation jar, which quickly became stuffed with cash. It was like a huge blessing for the community to witness right upon arrival.

There were some big-name bands and local artists that came down to be a part of Woodstick. Bands would come from Portland or Seattle to volunteer their time and each band played for at least one hour. They played all day, with different groups filling each time slot. Trespasser was a big band that played, and many more joined as this festival grew. Some other bands were: Duffy Bishop, The Pole Cats, Iguana Hat, The Robin Barrett Band, The No Land Band, and Sally and the Saddle-ites. They played a variety of music from country to jazz to pop. The main music during the event was rock and roll and blues. It was a delight to listen to.

As more families came in, I had a blast with the kids. I was like the Pied Piper, with a trail of kids following me everywhere I went. I made balloon animals, did sleight-of-hand magic, colored with the kids and always gave out hugs and my special stickers. There was a giant, wooden dance floor out in the field by the band. Many knew me from the Father/Daughter Dance, so when I started dancing, a crowd of kids rushed out to join me. Then other kids would see us, and it became a big to-do. We would laugh and dance for hours, even though I was exhausted. I would slip away if I could to rest my feet and drink water, before inevitably a child would find me and pull me back out to dance. I was so tired, but I really looked forward to each year.

At dusk families headed home, and I would finally sit to rest and enjoy the music. Mike only hired me to stay a couple of hours, but I donated the rest of my time to be there for the community. People do not believe how expensive it is to be a clown. The upkeep for my outfit, makeup, balloons, supplies, and tricks was costly each time Sparkle went out. Getting paid let me keep being Sparkle. Yet I always made sure that once those costs were met, Sparkle could go out and bless other people with the resources given to her.

I attended Woodstick as Sparkle for six or seven years. Because of his age, it became too hard for him to keep the event going.

Woodstick was a highly respected event by the community. Over the years, Mike received thousands of dollars in donations to buy instruments for kids in local schools who could not afford one. The food bank was overwhelmed by the amount of canned goods that were brought in to feed the community. This event became something everyone wanted to not only be a part of, but to give generously to as well. I was grateful and honored to be a part of this special event, change its image, and share in the joy it brought to the community.

Even a pause is part of
the journey.

CHAPTER 15

The Sad Goodbye

Rosemary and I were the best of partners. Our partnership was based upon fun, learning, teaching each other what we learned, and trust knowing that we had each other's back. The greatest part was honoring the Lord and trusting in Him.

We met together every week. Rosemary came to my house at night, and we practiced routines, shared sleight of hand magic, and learned new ways to enhance our skills. More importantly though, a deep friendship blossomed that took root in both of our hearts.

Our glittery and lively appearance made us inviting and safe. People came to know us as fun and loving to all. We were different from other clowns, especially with our calm and kind manner. Our reputation skyrocketed, and we were cherished by the community.

Many people asked me why I did not develop another character as well. I insisted that the Lord only wanted me to be Sparkle. He inspired and created Sparkle through me, and I honored that in every event that I did.

Other times people would ask why I did not disguise or alter my voice. I shared that the Lord wanted me to be authentic, even through Sparkle. I wanted people to realize that even though there is a person behind Sparkle, I am real and can be trusted. Sparkle is an extension of Cindy, and Cindy is an extension of Sparkle. We are one and the same!

My friendship with Rosemary grew in love and respect throughout the years. She sometimes did events on her own and I did too, but when the two of us were together, the house would rock with laughter. Together, we were on fire. We performed in California, Oregon, Idaho, Canada, and other places far from Walla Walla, Washington. Everything we did spread by word of mouth. The Lord let us go out there to use our skills as clowns to spread His love.

Despite our growing popularity, we were truly two humble clowns trying to share hope, joy, and a lot of love.

Every once in a while, Rosemary's daughter, Molly, would clown with us. It was always such a blessing when she did. She dressed as a tramp clown who did not speak except to us. Molly's attire included a sad-looking face, and she dressed as a hobo clown. Yet despite her muteness and initially off-putting appearance, Molly used great skill and talent to witness all of the love and joy that was inside of her. She made a powerful impression on the lives of others, and I think this avenue also led to some of her own internal healing as well.

Once, Rosemary and I worked a corporate event. We were Lacey and Sparkle, and I was excited to do another event with my partner. Throughout the day, Rosemary was distracted and sad. After the performance, she said we needed to talk. We walked out to my car, and Rosemary shared that this was her last event as Lacey. Rosemary's doctor told her that she was getting weak, and the effort and activity of being a clown irritated her lungs and was bad for her health. She could not be KC or Lacey ever again.

We hugged each other and wept. I could not imagine a life without my clown partner. I knew she had lung problems because she always had her inhaler with her, and towards the end of our six years working together, I knew her health was affected more. Yet this news still shook me hard.

Then Rosemary turned to me and said something incredibly powerful. "I think that God wants you to continue clowning by yourself."

I was shocked by her suggestion. We had spent years together in deep friendship and shared so many experiences and memories clowning together. I had done some events by myself, but for that to be the new normal was breaking my heart. It was hard to imagine people accepting just me. Just Sparkle. Yet Rosemary kept encouraging me. She said that I was incredible at spreading encouragement, joy, hope, and love all on my own. I did not need to worry because the Lord would be with me. What a gift her words were to me.

Despite her encouragement, Rosemary said she would not attend any parades, fairs or events that I was at. She knew that it would be too painful to see me as Sparkle, sharing the love and joy of clowning without being able to partake in it.

This was our final performance together, and Sparkle would never clown with KC or Lacey again. It was our final goodbye as partners.

Rosemary handed me a gift. I opened it and saw a beautiful letter written, "From Lacey, to Sparkle." It brought special encouragement to me when I was sad and missing my partner. I love to read it even now. She wrote it on an old-fashioned typewriter. The ink has faded gently over time, but I have the letter framed on my wall and the words with me still. I have it here now to share:

Sparkle

When I think of you
I think of Hope & Joy & Love.
A cheerful trusting soul
Close to our God above.
When others laugh and turn away
You reach out and draw them near.
All the lonely, hurting ones
Full of pain and bound by fear.
You caress them with your trust
And disarm them with your smile.
You give them Hope and Happiness
Not knowing all the while.
That they bless you in return
And give more than they take.
Where others look for wealth and fame
You do it for Christ's sake.
So I thank you for all that you are
You are real and not pretend.
I thank the Lord that I can say
I know you as my Friend.

Love Lacey 1991

I was so blessed to have had her for my partner. Through the rest of my clowning I was by myself. I could never have a partner like Rosemary. There were many people I helped train to be clowns and some who I grew very close to. One of these clowns was Wally Two-Hearts. We were great friends. We did many parades and events together, which brought me and the community a lot of joy. Yet my memories and partnership with Rosemary were something unique. The time we shared was something truly beautiful.

Unfortunately, Rosemary and I lost contact after she left clowning. Moving forward through the years, I tried to get in contact with her, but I never had any luck. Then another couple of years would go by, something would happen, and I would try again to find Rosemary but no luck. My heart would hurt because I had so much to say to her:

I wanted to thank you for talking with me at the Balloon Stampede all of those years ago and inviting me to my first clown workshop with Lil Petal.

I wanted to thank you for being the best partner I could have ever asked for. I wanted to thank you for all of the love and support, not to mention the laughter and tears!

Don't forget all of the learning that we shared and taught each other.

We had so much fun when we clowned together.

As I was writing this book, my friend and Angel Writer, Brittney, was going to see if she could find Rosemary for me. At the time of writing, today is August 22, 2025. I learned today that Rosemary passed away on August 22,

2010. Exactly fifteen years ago. My heart is heavy, but at least I have some closure.

Rosemary, I will always love you and be so grateful for all we shared as friends and partners. KC and Lacey, thank you for clowning with Sparkle. We had the best time ever!

You will always be missed in my heart!

Goodbye, My Dear Friend

Hope is the bridge between today and tomorrow.

CHAPTER 16

The 12-Step Retreat

Lake Coeur d'Alene is a glittering blue lake in northern Idaho surrounded by mountains and rich green vegetation like pine, spruce, and fir trees. It is a beautiful park, and I was invited, as Sparkle, to a 12-Step Retreat at a campsite on the lake. While it was too cold to go swimming, the view was still magnificent.

I shared a cabin with one of my friends, Gale. She is a lovely, bright person, and I was blessed to be her roommate.

We were at the retreat for two nights, and the second night was when I performed my program. During the day, I got to join in on the festivities and group sessions as myself. I met a lot of new people and listened to their stories. It was a privilege to be confided in.

The first night, my neck and shoulders were tight, and I had a pounding headache. Gale knew I was stressed, so she rubbed some eucalyptus oil on my shoulders and encouraged me. I slept great that night and woke up refreshed and grateful for such an intentional friendship.

One of my favorite parts of the day was our quiet time in the afternoon. During this time people could do whatever they wanted. Some people walked around the lake, some journaled under trees, some took a nap. Personally, I loved to walk and pray to the Lord. I felt His love in the swaying trees, the flying birds, the leaves on the ground, and the crisp scent of fall in the air. I prayed to the Lord and He gave me clarity about who I am in His love. I felt the Lord tell me to not be afraid when I performed that night. I knew He was with me and would give me the words to say.

The people at the retreat knew I was going to do the program, but only Gale and a few others knew what it would entail.

The program was to start right after dinner. While everyone was eating, I was in the bathroom getting ready to be Sparkle. They saved me dinner for afterwards since it took so long. Then it was time for the show.

To start the performance, I was introduced as Sparkle. When the announcer handed me the mic, I broke into a smile. I always have fun when a mic is in my hand.

Even when I was growing up, I was the bubbly one of my sisters. Any time I had a mic, they could not get it back.

The people at the retreat were from all over the country, not just Walla Walla. Some people had heard of Sparkle and were excited, but many had not heard of me before.

To loosen up the group, I started with some sleight of hand tricks. This caused the group to laugh and be at ease. Then I moved on to some tricks that incorporated messages of hope and not giving up. Those messages were special to me because I adjusted them to fit whatever group function I was in. I did messages of hope for drug addicts and alcoholics. People suffering from eating disorders and depression were given words of life, and those in a mental health crisis were encouraged. These messages touched everyone, even myself. My experiences with physical and emotional trauma allowed me to not only be vulnerable but also to speak from a place of healing. Hope is available for everyone, and the Lord is there for each person who opens their heart to Him.

The Lord's presence was in that room, filling everyone with promises of hope, forgiveness, acceptance, encouragement and most notably, love.

When I had finished, there was not a dry eye in the room as each person was touched so deeply. It was God's message to me too. The Lord was again so amazing. I just had to remember that if I did my part, He would do His.

Learn from Yesterday
Live for Today
Hope for Tomorrow

CHAPTER 17

Bullying

When Sparkle started becoming popular, different organizations, churches, hospitals, and schools reached out to Sparkle to come and give a message. One of my favorite places to visit was the schools. They usually wanted me to talk, visit, and do some fun things through tricks and entertainment. They also asked me to share messages through sleight of hand magic while telling a story against bullying and offering hope and healing to kids. I worked with children of all ages, and loved to hug them goodbye when I left.

One year I was asked to perform at Adams School. Back around 2016-2017, the population of Adams, Oregon was only 389, so you can imagine how small the classrooms were at the schools in Adams. When I was asked to perform, they wanted me to do it for the whole K-12 school. They wanted me to do three shows in the auditorium. The first one was for kindergarten through fifth graders, and that one went really well. Some of the kids knew me and were excited to see me. I did a few little tricks with their help to engage them, and made a few balloon animals. Then I put a fifteen-inch needle through a balloon (without it popping) while telling the children the importance of being prepared. The kids also loved the message of the 'Broken Heart' and how I presented it. To finish I mimed the song "I Believe" and "When You Walk Through a Storm". All of the kids came up to give me a hug, and then I quickly prepared for the next group.

The sixth, seventh, and eighth graders came in next. I did pretty much the same thing as I did for the younger classes, but a little bit more in depth with the messages that I was sharing. It was a good presentation, with a time for questions and answers at the end, and then they all went back to class.

The grades that I was most concerned with were the ninth, tenth, eleventh and twelfth graders. I was dreading the high schoolers. I was worried that I might get a lot of heckling from them because they were the oldest group of kids. But you know what, the good Lord really has an awesome sense of humor.

I had an amazing time with all of the classes, but these older kids were the best! I had all of my props, things for my messages, and my music on a table so when the kids came into the auditorium some laughed and others wanted to know what was going on. They were excited to see me. I started laughing and told them that I was there to talk about bullying, but also just to be me. I wanted to be real with them.

I first introduced myself as Sparkle the Clown, and I told the kids that we were going to have some fun. I went right into a few tricks with their help, which got the attention of the kids. Then I asked for two strong guys to come join me. When they came on the little stage, I had a bag of balloons and told each one to pick a balloon and to blow it up as big or as little as they wanted and tie it off. They did that, and then I did the same. Then I said that if they were really careful, I would let them put a fifteen inch needle through their balloon.

My needle was extremely sharp, so they had to be very careful with it. Each guy could try and put the needle through the balloon that they picked out for themselves. I even had a silver thread hanging from the needle so they could see the needle go through the balloon. Each boy tried but then the balloon would pop. Finally it was my turn. I picked up my balloon and I told everyone that my balloon was smaller than theirs because my hands were smaller and I needed to hold onto my balloon. While I was talking, I picked up a cloth and rubbed it a few times on my needle. Then I began. As I put the needle through the balloon, I gave a message on being prepared. If they wanted to succeed in life, then they had to be prepared by studying for their tests, working hard in practice, applying for jobs and aiming towards their dreams. I said it was important for them to do the best job possible at whatever they were doing. Even if it was doing the dishes, their goal should be to be the best dishwasher ever.

As I gave my talk, they watched the needle go clean through the balloon. When it came out the other side, I smiled and popped the balloon. Glitter that was in the balloon rained down onto the stage. I told them that I was prepared because I first wiped down the needle with a little bit of oil on my cloth, and I knew where to put the needle through the balloon to give it the best chance of not popping. I was prepared! I had to blow up the balloon to the right size so I could hold it. Then I had to know where to push the needle through – near the bottom where the latex is thickest. The rags helped the needle slide through cleanly, and the eye of the needle had a sparkly thick thread so the kids could see it. Finally, I popped the balloon at the end so they would know that it was real.

I also told them that sometimes the balloons pop early, before I am done. No matter how prepared someone is, sometimes things do not work out and that's okay too. In life there are always lessons to be learned.

Then I did a few fun tricks and we were all laughing. Next came one of my favorite messages, "The Torn Heart".

I lifted up a heart cut out of paper and I told the kids, "Some days we get up and our hearts feel this big, and that everything is going great. But then things happen to us that are out of our control. Maybe you studied really hard for a big test that you needed to pass, but you blew it. Maybe your pet died. Maybe your parents are going through a divorce and that tears at your heart."

While talking, I was ripping and tearing the heart apart in front of the kids. Then I crumble up the heart in my hands and walk out to the crowd.

"But when you have been touched by someone who really loves you and cares about you, like your parents, a special teacher, grandparents, or good friends." Here I stopped and held out my hands with the torn heart inside for several of the kids to touch the shredded pieces. "Then it allows the Lord to come into our heart and work miracles."

"Remember the heart that was torn and hurting." I closed my fists and then opened my hands. "It is now made whole again."

Then I lifted up the heart that was put back together, without any tears in it. They were impressed!

Next, I showed the students two blue scarves that looked the same and gave them to two different kids. I asked them to drop the scarves in my bag. Then I told them how important it is to be yourself, and sometimes being different is good. A student then reached into the bag and pulled out the two scarves. One was still blue, but the other had white dots on it.

Finally, I shared how hurtful and harmful bullying was. My message was really impactful for the kids after seeing the creative ways I taught and cared for them.

At the end was a time for questions and answers. They could ask me any question about Sparkle, and I would answer them honestly. Surprisingly, it was the guys that asked me the most questions. Some of their main questions were:

Why did I get started in clowning?

How did I pick my name?

Are there clown schools?

Did I go to clown school?

I shared how the Lord has shown me everything that I am supposed to do. This is my ministry. I have a calling to give hope, encouragement, and above all, love.

I finished the program by doing the routine "I Believe" and "When You Walk Through A Storm." I used sign language and miming to bring the routine to life. At the end of the song, both the high school boys and girls had tears in their eyes. It was the perfect way to conclude the performance.

The students stood and gave Sparkle a standing ovation. That group will forever be in my heart, as my time with them was so meaningful and memorable.

The whole day was very moving and I felt so blessed. I knew that the Lord was smiling down on us.

Any time I did a performance, whether it was for a birthday party, school, or public function, I prayed that the Lord would use my performance to touch them. No matter what a person was going through, I wanted God to work through me and help them.

At every event there was at least one person, sometimes multiple people, who were deeply hurting. They needed a hug or someone to listen to them and show them compassion.

Sometimes I would interact with people who were dirty or smelled poorly and all they wanted was a hug, which I gladly gave. The Lord used me and worked through me in so many different ways.

"For I know the plans
and thoughts I have for you,"
declares the Lord, "plans for peace
and well-being, and not for
disaster, to give you a
future and a hope."
- Jeremiah 29:11

CHAPTER 18

Beauty on the Dance Floor

An event that I looked forward to participating in every year was the annual Father/Daughter Banquet. Each year it was held at Elk's Lodge, the Wednesday before Valentine's Day. The first time I attended as Sparkle, I did not know what to expect. While fathers and daughters sat around tables and enjoyed a meal together, I walked around, introduced myself, and spoke with families. I tried to make it to as many tables as I could to hand out my *I Hugged A Clown Today!* stickers.

It was really sweet seeing all of the fathers, young and old, with their daughters. Some young fathers were there with infant daughters. There were fathers with teenagers, and fathers with their daughters and granddaughters.

Over time, there were a couple of families that I grew close to and anticipated seeing each year. One family was an Italian family where the patriarch was in his late eighties. He would bring his daughters, granddaughters, and great-granddaughters. He was an outstanding man and extremely proud of the women in his family. This man had one of the first wineries in the area and was well-established in the community. I was his banker, and whenever he saw me at these dances, he would always ask me how his money was doing. Which he was not supposed to do since that night I was Sparkle, not his banker.

Yet I loved his family. His daughters, in their sixties, would always thank me for making this such a special event. I was their banker too, so I had known them for a long time. They appreciated how much I had done for their dad to make this event come to life for him and his daughters, granddaughters, and great-granddaughters. I cherished the relationship I had with this family.

There was one western couple that loved to dance. They would swing and whirl gracefully across the floor. It was a gift to watch them. After each song they would hug, and it was special to witness their connection and love through dance.

After the meal, dessert was brought out, the band set up, and the dance floor was prepared. I have never seen such tender emotions as when fathers would escort their daughters onto the dance floor. The young girls would gaze up at their fathers, while the men looked down on their sweet girls with adoration. The shared look of love in their eyes was like magic. Sometimes they would sway back and forth, while other times they would do a special dance they had practiced together.

Fathers and daughters would do this for a couple of songs, and then the men would sit down to socialize. That was my time to shine, because then Sparkle would go out on the dance floor. The kids wanted to dance with Sparkle song after song. Sometimes we would create a big circle so all of the girls could join. Other times we would all hold hands and swing around the dance floor.

The fathers watched on contentedly, grateful to see their daughters laughing and spinning across the room. They loved seeing how much fun their daughters were having with Sparkle.

About forty-five minutes into the dancing, we took a break to announce winners from the raffle prize. I got to bring three girls on stage and MC the event, which was great because it meant I got to be on the microphone.

I introduced the girls and let them pick the winners of the drawing. I gave the girls gifts for helping, and then we were back on the dance floor.

As the event concluded, I talked to fathers as they got ready to leave. Some would share their feelings as a first-time dad, with their baby girl strapped in a carrier. Others shared the joy of dancing with their teenage daughters. I did this event for about eight years. I would see girls who danced on their fathers' toes turn into teenagers. The little girls became young ladies and young dads grew into comfortable fathers. It was such a blessing to see them grow up. Through the years, the way fathers and daughters would dance together might have evolved, but that was what made it beautiful. The father was her protector and would always be there for her. She might not be stepping on his toes anymore, but his love for her was radiant. I loved watching the little girls grow up.

By the end of the night I was exhausted from the hours on my feet and dancing. Yet I would not have changed it for the world.

Never give up. Today is hard. Tomorrow will be worse, but the day after tomorrow will be sunshine.

CHAPTER 19

The Re-Grand Opening of Silver Saddle

One of the most important days of my life was when Sparkle came out and performed at my stepsister's wedding in California City. While I mentioned that wonderful story of acceptance from my town and family earlier in this book, I want to remind the reader of the significance of the wedding's location: my sister and her husband's resort, Silver Saddle Ranch and Club.

Silver Saddle was an incredible natural getaway on the outskirts of California City. Linda and Jim were part-owners with two other people. Together, they created a space that became a wonderful attraction, bringing people from all over the country together. Silver Saddle spread across acres of land, featuring lodges and rooms, long sweeping pathways, walking trails, ponds, and fountains. Adventurous activities like kayaking and horseback riding drew thrill-seekers, while families with kids enjoyed the petting zoo and nature walks. For those seeking to relax, the resort offered massages, manicures, pedicures, and tanning beds.

Many years after the wedding and embracing Sparkle publicly within our community as Sparkle to our community, part of Silver Saddle caught on fire. Although the fire was an accident, it devastated the community. Linda and Jim faced many challenges as they navigated the rebuilding process.

When it was time to officially reopen, Silver Saddle insisted that Sparkle the Clown attend. It was advertised in the local newspaper that I would be a part of the re-grand opening, and many people from California City were excited to see me again.

Silver Saddle was packed with people from California City, LA County, and even some visitors from Arizona. I was thrilled that Linda and Jim had a huge turnout.

I arrived at my sister's house on Thursday, and the re-grand opening ran Friday and Saturday from the morning until early evening. It was exciting to see how everyone would react to Sparkle now that it had been several years since they had seen me perform at the wedding reception. I was nervous, too, wondering if I would still be accepted. This was the town where we grew up, and as one of the first families in that area, everyone knew us. Many new people would also be attending, so I hoped that the joy of Sparkle would remain evident throughout the weekend.

Linda had fun driving around in her little Smurf Mobile, which is what we called her decked-out golf cart. My younger sister was even shorter than me, around four feet eight inches tall, and everyone, including her husband, referred to her as "Smurfette." Despite her small stature, Linda was tough as nails with a bright spark of life in her.

The Smurf Mobile was the cutest little golf cart I had ever seen. It was off-white with a purple stripe wrapped around the cart. The sides featured pink and purple stripes, and Smurfette was painted on both of the doors. It was perfect for her, and she loved it. Linda and Jim had a beautiful house next to Silver Saddle, so the Smurf Mobile helped them access both properties easily.

When Linda told me that I could spend the weekend driving the Smurf Mobile around the event, I was delighted. This was the perfect mode of transportation for Sparkle.

When I came out as Sparkle, everyone was excited to see me and I was excited to see them as well. I drove that little Smurf Mobile all over the resort visiting with kids, making balloon animals, giving out hug stickers, performing sleight of hand magic, and simply listening to the older kids who wanted to talk about what was going on in their lives. For them, it was important that I be present and listen to them while they talked, and sometimes I helped dry their tears.

I had so much fun being Sparkle at Silver Saddle again. The weekend was a great success for Linda and Jim and I was so happy to be a part of that experience.

Seriously—humor can help your mental and physical health

What's so funny?

Pick a joke, any joke:

▶ *Why did the scientist remove his doorbell?* Answer: To win a Nobel Prize.

▶ Outside of a dog, a book is man's best friend. Inside of a dog, it's too dark to read.

▶ How do trains hear? Answer: With their engineers.

A growing number of health professionals say a little laughter can help you feel better. They believe humor is good for our mental and physical health.

Steven Sultanoff, Ph.D., doesn't just think humor matters *in our lives*, it's the name of his Web site: *www.humormatters.com*. He's a psychologist, president of the American Association for Therapeutic Humor, and a self-described "mirthologist."

"There aren't a lot of studies on humor and health," he says, in part because it's hard to measure. "We can observe laughter and what happens to us biochemically when we laugh, but [how do we measure] the emotional experience, the cognitive experience of humor?"

Research has discovered a few things about laughter's effect on health, says Dr. Sultanoff:

▶ Laughter increases production of certain antibodies that fight some types of infection (especially upper respiratory).

▶ Laughter decreases production of stress-related hormones.

▶ Laughter appears to increase tolerance to pain.

EMOTIONAL BOOST

Most people would agree that a sense of humor is good for one's mental health.

But what does that mean? Exactly what is "humor"?

Dr. Sultanoff breaks humor into three parts:

1 Wit, the thought-oriented experience.

2 Mirth, the emotional experience.

3 Laughter, the physical experience.

You don't need all three to be amused, Dr. Sultanoff says. But the most powerful humor experience comes when they combine.

So what can humor do for us mentally?

Dr. Sultanoff lists the following psychological benefits:

▶ Humor helps us relate to other people.

▶ Humor reduces stress.

▶ It replaces distressing emotions with positive ones. Have you ever tried to stay mad after laughing?

HUMOR IN THE HOSPITAL

Ruth Hamilton doesn't need any convincing about humor's effect on health. She founded the Carolina Health and Humor Association ("Carolina Ha Ha") and developed the Laugh Mobile.

Volunteers take the Laugh Mobile—a cart filled with tapes, books, clowning props and other items—into hospitals and other health care settings. Hamilton has seen people in chemotherapy "fight back" with water pistols, and doctors banter with patients over the finer points of a rubber chicken.

HUMOR REPLACES NEGATIVE EMOTIONS WITH POSITIVE ONES.

"We have people who have put themselves into intensive humor therapy [who] did feel physical relief because of it," says Hamilton, who has traveled to Russia with famed funny physician Patch Adams.

HUMOR YOURSELF

To incorporate more humor into your life, Dr. Sultanoff offers the following *suggestions*:

▶ Read at *least one joke* a day.

▶ *Listen to humorous tapes while driving.*

▶ Put wind-ups or other small toys at your desk. Fellow workers will probably want to play with them too.

▶ Wear a humorous article of clothing, such as a Looney Tune tie or funny-looking pin.

▶ Carry props with you. Dr. Sultanoff blows bubbles when stuck in traffic, and has been known to don a red clown nose without warning.

So laugh a little—or laugh a lot. There really are benefits to seeing the lighter side of life.

"For many are called (invited, summoned), but few are chosen."
–Matthew 22:14

CHAPTER 20

A Magazine Article on Joy - Featuring Sparkle!

Coffey Communications was a major business in Walla Walla that provided content for health magazines to use and publish nationally and globally. They had articles relating to all aspects of health and provided photos to accompany each piece. Since they distributed information internationally, they offered a variety of photos for magazines to choose from. For example, if the article was about running, Coffey Communications would provide multiple photo options of people running. Then magazines could choose people of different ages, genders or ethnicities to fit their target demographic.

As myself, Cindy, my photo was used many times, but I never saw the articles in print. Yet there was one article I did see, and that was the one featuring Sparkle the Clown.

In the November 2001 *Health Science Magazine*, National Edition, the whole magazine was based on the joy of laughter. Sparkle was invited to pose in pictures for their primary article called, "What's So Funny." I was thrilled. Coffey Communications paid me quite well to attend this photo shoot, which I was grateful for. After my tithe to the church, I spent the rest of the money on replenishing the supplies needed to maintain Sparkle.

The photo shoot was such a fun and exciting experience. I felt like a model as the photographers had me try different poses. I had pictures taken with people of two different ethnicities so that the international magazines could use the photos that best aligned with their audience.

While all of these health magazines had many photos to choose from to accompany this article on joy, 70% chose Sparkle for their magazine.

I was grateful that this article was written and so popular in health magazines because laughter is for everyone.

The following are some quotes from the article, along with some of my own thoughts and suggestions.

* * *

Find one thing to laugh about every day.

Laughing alleviates distressing emotions and replaces them with positive feelings. How can you be angry with someone when you just finished laughing with them?

Remember, a pet is a wonderful companion to have. They reduce stress by giving unconditional love and they just want to feel that they are loved back. When they do something wrong and you have to discipline them, they always have a forgiving heart.

Pick a joke, any joke:

Why did the scientist remove his doorbell?

To win a Nobel Prize

Outside of a dog, a book is man's best friend.

Inside of a dog, it's too dark to read.

How do trains hear?

With their engineers.

I know that these jokes were old ones but didn't you smile?

Many health professionals believe humor is good for our emotional and physical health.

It lifts our spirits and fills us with hope and joy!

What does humor actually do for us?

Humor helps us relate to other people.

Humor reduces stress.

Humor replaces distressing emotions with positive ones.

Humor yourself:

Read at least one joke a day.

Listen to funny tapes while driving.

Carry props with you.

(Dr. Sultanoff blows bubbles when stuck in traffic, and has been known to put on a red clown nose without warning.)

So laugh a little – or laugh a lot, and enjoy the benefits of the lighter side of life.

* * *

Coffey Communications is an amazing company because of all that they do to share health information that everyone can benefit from. Being a part of this magazine was a way for me to share God's love with more people. There are so many hurtful people and experiences in the world, but a person always has control of themself and how they respond. Each person matters. Each person is important. If I could be a part of showing people internationally how much love and joy they could find and create in the world, then that truly was the greatest gift I could share through this article.

Smiles are for Life

To learn more about the mission of Smiles for Life or to make a tax-deductible contribution, visit our website at www.SmilesAreForLife.org.

The Joy and Cheer of a Clown

It is the mission of Smiles for Life to encourage, rally, show the love of Jesus, and put smiles on the faces of all people, including those who are suffering with loneliness, fear and anxiety, and the stress of life, through the joy and cheer of a clown.

Humor : Skits : Story Telling

Sparkle the Clown, 2010

Smiles for Life works to achieve their mission by using humor, skits, and story telling among many other avenues. The organization concentrates the majority of its outreach to hospitals, churches, and community events by participating regularly in local parades, programs and county fairs so to bring awareness to the organization's mission and purpose.

"Find a place inside where there's joy, and the joy will burn out the pain."

Joseph Campbell

CHAPTER 21

The Beginning of Smiles For Life

For twenty-five years I had helped people as Sparkle, and I started wondering what would happen when I could no longer be Sparkle. I was really worried about Sparkle because Sparkle did not define Cindy, Cindy defined Sparkle. We are an extension of each other: Cindy was Sparkle and Sparkle was Cindy.

Around 2010, I decided to start a nonprofit foundation called "Smiles For Life." I thought of all the work I had done as Sparkle, and all the lives I was able to touch. Perhaps this work could continue through other people who wanted to reach out to the hurting, depressed, sick, scared, and lonely. They could also share love with all of the joyful, excited, and happy people too.

These people did not have to be clowns. They could be storytellers, jugglers, therapy pet owners, or anything their heart desired. They could even be someone who just wants to hold someone's hand. It did not matter to me, as long as they cared and reached out to help others.

There are always people who need support. Someone might be getting ready for surgery or coming home from the hospital. Someone might be without a place to live or wondering where their next meal will come from. There are people who are getting a divorce or whose spouse is dying. Whatever one's situation, I have found that people are desperate for a hand to hold. Through Smiles for Life, there could be an angel ready to help and share love with someone who was hurting.

This foundation would be filled with encouragement, hope, joy and above all, love. I wanted others to see the love of Jesus through all of us.

I had my board filled with incredible people, and I got my 501(c)(3) status for Smiles for Life. We had our board meetings, and our dreams looked like they were becoming a reality. Unfortunately, Smiles for Life did not last as long as I had hoped. After hurtful deceit and greed by someone I knew, Smiles for Life closed, but the nine months that we were running, a wonderful impact was made.

One of my favorite stories happened right after Smiles for Life got started.

It was close to Christmas, and Pearl (who was also my secretary on the board) wanted to go with me to visit all of the patients at the hospital. Carrie and Kittie (who were also on the board) decided they would bake all different kinds of homemade cookies. They got other friends to join them in their baking so that we could give out the best plate of cookies ever.

Now here is the kicker, we wanted to do this on Christmas Eve, which was only two days away. All of us worked and still had to get our own homes in order for Christmas as well. The foundation had just started a few months prior, and we were all new at this. We leaned heavily on each other for help, guidance, and support. Yet we were thrilled to let everyone know that Smiles for Life was here, and we were going to do our very best.

On Christmas Eve, I got off work, went home, and got ready as Sparkle. Pearl also got dressed up. She fixed herself up as an elf, Sparkle's partner. We met at Carrie's house where they had all of the cookie trays ready for us to deliver.

There were about seventy-five trays of beautiful cookies. I brought stuffed animals to give to any children we met at the hospital. We had an awesome team, and I was delighted that they were on board for Smiles for Life.

As we drove towards the hospital, Pearl and I prayed that the Lord would lead us and guide us through this magical night. We asked the Lord to work through us and bless all of the patients that we would come in contact with. We asked the Lord to let everyone feel Him through our touch, our voice, and our hugs. We asked that everyone accept the gift of peace that we were offering through our Lord and Savior, Jesus Christ.

First we stopped at the nursing home, Pioneer House. There was a special family that I always liked to visit when I was Sparkle. Arnie lived there and received care, and his wife, Harriet, visited him frequently. They were both dear to my heart. Arnie was in the early stages of Alzheimer's, so I wanted to see him as much as possible while he remembered me. Harriet was always with him, and she helped him to be calm and relaxed. Their beautiful daughter, Paula, moved down from Leavenworth to help take care of both her mom and dad.

I was excited to see this family, especially since the Lord gave me a very special gift: even though Arnie had a hard time remembering things, he never forgot me. He remembered me as Cindy and Sparkle.

Harriet was in the room with Arnie, and they were having a nice afternoon together. When we walked in, the smiles on both of their faces were priceless. We gave them a tray of cookies, and Pearl and I sat and visited for a little bit. Harriet and I talked about how she was holding up and I listened as she talked. I made Arnie a couple of balloon animals. His favorite was the giraffe, so I always made sure he always got one. Harriet asked if we could stop by her house because her whole family was down for Christmas, and they were all at her house right then. We immediately agreed!

Harriet's family was surprised by the arrival of a clown and elf on their front porch, but they quickly welcomed us in to hang out and socialize. We had a wonderful time visiting with everyone, but it was soon time for us to continue on our way and go to the hospital.

At the hospital, we had the best time with the patients, kids, and staff members. We had so much fun with the nurses at the desks, but the real fun was when we went into the rooms. The smiles on their faces were priceless and the ones that could eat cookies really lit up, especially when they saw the beautiful mixture on the plate. We were at the hospital for hours and gave out all of our trays of cookies and a few stuffed animals.

For some people, Christmas is the loneliest time of year. There are people who are alone or are missing a family member who has passed away. At the hospital, there were people working and not with their families. There were people who were sick, hopeless and alone. Pearl and I felt that if we could put a smile on their faces, then being there for all hours of the night was well worth it, and trust me, it was! The joy, encouragement, hope, and love were felt powerfully in every room.

We sat and listened to their stories, laughed with them, and even got tears in our eyes at times. I did a magic trick with my message of hope and not giving up, but the majority of the time Sparkle and her elf buddy shared LOVE with everyone we met. Then, with the patient's permission, we would pray for them.

We went from room to room like this, but each time we felt in our hearts that there were more people that the Lord wanted us to see.

We typically entered a room together, but if it seemed there was a strong connection with only one of us and the patient really needed to talk, the other one would quietly slip out and let them have time alone. We wanted it to be a special time for the patient. Pearl and I each had meaningful moments with individual patients that we cherish to this day.

Here are my most notable memories:

Pearl and I went into one of the rooms where a young lady was hurting terribly. She connected with me and kept sharing her story, so I stayed after Pearl left.

This lady was a young mother who just had surgery. Needless to say, she was hurting pretty bad. She was upset and depressed, so I just sat and listened. When she was finished talking, I prayed over her for peace and healing. Then I left and caught up with Pearl. We continued room to room listening and praying for the patients.

I knew there were still a few people in the hospital who needed to know that the Lord was with them and would never leave them. It was getting late, but we knew God had more work for us to do.

As we walked into this one room, an older man was lying in bed. When he rolled over and saw us standing there, his face lit up. He took my hand as I introduced myself and Pearl. I knew in my heart that this man was someone the Lord wanted me to connect with and pray for. Pearl went to the next room and I sat on the edge of his bed while we talked.

The man shared that he had seen me for many, many years but thought that he would never be able to talk to me – and yet, there I was. I held his hand and said, "Yes. God is so good." Then I listened to his story. By the end, we both had tears streaming down our faces. I prayed for him and he prayed for me as well. I gave him a big hug and a *I Hugged A Clown Today!* sticker before I left. I was touched by our time together.

As Pearl and I were getting ready to leave and go home, I still had a feeling that the Lord had one more person for me to see.

We walked down a corridor. I looked to my left and there she was. A young mother sat on a bed, murmuring to a little baby wrapped up in a crib. The baby was tiny and looked very sick. The young mother herself appeared thin, ill and anxious. I asked if I could sit down with her for a while, and she said yes. I do not think that she had showered in many days, but I held her close as she cried.

She shared that she was not in a good relationship. I did not know if it was with the baby's dad or not, but I told her that she did the right thing by bringing her little one into the ER. I was shocked when she told me that her little boy was actually a few years old. His little body was not doing well and was possibly shutting down. Child Protective Services had been called and now it was likely that her little boy would be taken away.

The young mom said that she was leaving the man. I told her that I knew that was hard and I was so proud of her. She said that her little boy was all she cared about. She also told me that she was a good mother and always put her son first. As we talked, I pulled out one of my props and played with the little boy. He really liked it, so I gave it to him. While the boy played, I told his mom, "God is right here with us. He has never left you, and He loves you so much." Then we prayed.

By the end of the evening, I was exhausted both mentally and physically. Throughout the whole night I kept questioning the Lord, "How did you care for so many people?" Jesus witnessed to hundreds of people at a time, and He kept doing more.

You know what he told me?

"Just care for one person at a time. Share *LOVE* and *KINDNESS*. It will get done."

It will all fall into place.

You know what? Jesus was right. If we looked at the whole hospital, then we would have felt overwhelmed. If we took it one person at a time, we would make it to everyone and have amazing stories to share.

Pearl had special memories from that evening as well.

When Pearl and I went to the Pioneer House, and then to Harriet's home, it touched Pearl's heart in a special way.

I believe that the Lord was getting her ready for a magical night of miracles and blessings.

When we got to the hospital, Pearl allowed me to pray for both of us as we spread joy, happiness, encouragement, and the love of the Lord. I really wanted Pearl to feel and see the miracles that were happening around her. It is in giving from the heart that we receive blessings as well.

The nurses said that there were no kids in the hospital, because they were able to let them go home to be with their families for Christmas. Since all of the kids were gone, they said that we could go anywhere in the hospital except where they had one inmate. That was fine with us because we did not really want to run into the inmate anyway.

We went into our first room. To our dismay, there was a young man in there that had been in a motorcycle accident. His legs were in traction, slowly pulling ligaments and bones back together. Bandages were all over his body, and he was hooked to several monitors. The young man was in a lot of pain but also severely sad. There were some family members with him in the room. We did not stay long, but we wanted him to know that we were there for him.

In the next room was a sweet old lady. She lived in Florida but came up to spend the holidays with her family. She had fallen on the ice and broken her shoulder. The old lady was in so much pain and filled with a deep sadness in her heart. Her family had gone back home, and now she was alone. I took her hand and asked if I could pray for her, to which she said yes.

Pearl stayed with her for a while and they had a nice visit. Pearl gave her so much peace and love by just listening. It was helpful for Pearl to give peace to this old woman, but Pearl received an even greater blessing of being able to sit and spend time with her. We visited patients until 1:00 a.m., enjoying special moments with each person. Years later, Pearl told me that it was her most memorable Christmas. She saw the Lord work in so many wonderful ways.

It was something that she would never forget.

We should not let our fears hold us back from pursuing our hopes.
-John F Kennedy

CHAPTER 22

The Next 10 Years

There was so much joy and fun over the next ten years, but I was starting to have a few concerns. My spine was coming down and pressing on my heart and lungs. It was making me short of breath, and I was shrinking. I am now four feet six inches, and kids loved the fact that many of them were taller than me. Even the four- and five-year-olds would measure themselves against me. We always joked and laughed because many of the kids I knew from a very young age, and now they were tall, beautiful teenagers.

Sometimes when I would be at an event, I would see someone hurting and sad. I would go over to see if they were okay. Many times the person was a teenage girl, who was dealing with emotional stress. She would ask if I could sit down and talk with her. Of course I said YES.

I would sit with her as long as it took for her to share what was on her heart. All I did was listen. When she was finished, she felt better. She just needed to share her story to a nonthreatening person who would listen and reveal to her how loved and valued she truly was. Moments like these were significant to me because I felt purposeful and hopeful in my work as a clown.

Unfortunately, many events arose during this time that limited my ability to be Sparkle. In 2014, I had knee replacement surgery on my right knee. The surgery went smoothly, even though I had to rest and recover for many weeks. In the fall of 2015, I had knee replacement surgery on my left knee. The recovery was unexpectedly painful and complicated. I was in rehab for three and a half months. Cartilage kept building up in my knee where it was not supposed to. I had a great team of doctors and physical therapists, but my knee was not healing properly. My doctor checked with other specialist doctors in this field, and they said they had only seen the condition of my knee post-surgery once or twice in their careers. It was a slow and painful process physically, but I also had a great deal of sadness emotionally as Sparkle could not go out and be a light like she normally was. These knee surgeries were just one of the many setbacks during this time.

Another event arose during these years that broke my heart: scary clowns were going out, hurting and scaring people. They were destroying the beauty and love of true clowns.

Scary clowns were people who purposefully dressed in grotesque costumes with fear-inducing makeup. They threatened and scared adults and children for sport. Some scary clowns tried to lure children into the woods away from their family. Some chased or hurt people. This phenomenon was spreading across the United States, and the rising fear of scary clowns appeared across the news.

It made me angry when all of this started because scary clowns even started appearing in Walla Walla. Despite the rising fear, I still kept serving and performing as Sparkle because I knew that the Lord would protect me.

When the Christmas Lighting Parade came, the social fear of clowns was at an all-time high. For the Christmas Parade, event coordinators said that clowns were banned from entry. There was fear of what type of clowns would show up, and people and children in the community were afraid of clowns in public spaces.

While at a Christmas Bazaar, I ran into one of my friends, Shane, who was one of the main people working for the Walla Walla Downtown Foundation. He asked me if I would join the Christmas Parade. I told him that I thought clowns were not allowed. Shane said that I was the only clown that they wanted and would be allowed in the parade. Many people in the community knew me, and I could be a blessing to the families that attended. Shane said that they wanted me to show people that Sparkle was still here, standing in for "good against evil". I had a lot to consider, and I needed to talk to my family about all of this. I told him that I would call him on Monday and let him know.

I was nervous to commit to the parade. There were stories in the news of scary clowns being arrested, people dying, and citizens fighting back against the scary clowns. Because of this, I did not want someone to be afraid of me and hurt me out of fear of me or my intentions.

All weekend I prayed about the event, and I felt that I needed to support our community by being in the parade. My husband and daughter were concerned for my safety and asked me not to participate. Yet the conviction in my heart grew stronger, and I knew what I needed to do. I called Shane on Monday morning and told him that I would do it. I was all in.

I knew the Lord would keep me safe and protected. I just needed to continue to trust Him.

I called my friend Eddie. He said that he would drive me in his side-by-side ATV, so I would not be walking and could be safe. Eddie and his family were always there to help me whenever an occasion arose. I felt so blessed and loved by his whole family.

My daughter, Jenni, was nervous for me to be out in public as Sparkle, but I kept telling her that everything would be all right. With this great fear of clowns, I knew that I needed to be there for the community and show them there still are good clowns and I was not going anywhere.

When the parade started, excitement grew and fear fell away. People started clapping and hollering my name as we drove by so that I would see them. Kids even ran up to the ATV just to get a hug and say that they loved me.

It was such a fun parade, and when it was over, I realized that nothing happened to me or anyone else in the parade. I thanked the Lord and was so grateful that everyone was safe.

Happy is he who learns to bear what he cannot change! -J.C.F.von Schiller

CHAPTER 23

My Last Parade

In July of 2016, I was hit by a driver who ran a red light. I was driving from Walla Walla to College Place. Turning left out of the bank, I drove along Alder Street. I was stopped at a red light in the right lane, with a huge vehicle in the left lane, blinker on and waiting to turn left.

The light turned green.

The vehicle on my left started pulling forward, momentarily blocking my view of any danger as I proceeded straight. I saw the car right before he hit me.

The car running the red light slammed into my driver's side without even braking. His car flipped twice before landing upside down and sliding across the road.

I'll never forget the paramedics saying that if he had hit me just twelve inches further back, I would not have made it. Yet the Lord's angels protected me.

My left front panel, fender and driver's side door were crushed. I was severely injured in the accident.

I had finally recovered from my knee replacement surgeries when the accident occurred. I had been back at work since February using a cane, and in late spring, Sparkle was able to go out and perform again. Now, though, my entire body was devastated. Even as I slowly recovered over the years, I no longer had the strength in my arms to hold youngsters who were often given to me for photo opportunities. My left leg was deeply pained, so I had trouble bending my leg or kneeling down.

I was desperately afraid of dropping a little child, and I could no longer bend down to get on eye level with them. That saddened me so much inside.

I grieved because I knew that it was time for Sparkle to step away from the magical role that she had played for so many decades.

My wonderful daughter kindly helped me with this process of letting go. Jennifer talked to me about everything. She encouraged me in all of the wonderful things that I had done as Sparkle. She gently reminded me of my physical pain, and how it was unsafe for me (and unsafe for the kids) if I continued. Jennifer listened to me and showed me great compassion as I struggled with this decision.

I decided to do my last parade as Sparkle in August of 2019. My final appearance would be at the Walla Walla Fair and Frontier Days Parade.

Before the parade, there was a beautiful article written about Sparkle in the newspaper. It shared some of my story through the years and said that I would be hanging up my pink glittery shoes due to health reasons. The article noted that my last parade would be that Saturday.

The morning of the parade, I was overwhelmed with emotions. After thirty-five years of sharing love and joy as Sparkle, this would be my last parade.

My good friend Skeeter fixed up his pearl white convertible so that I could sit propped atop the back of it for the parade. I felt like a princess sitting back there, waving at my friends and community. I was grateful to him for his kindness in honoring me and celebrating me in this way. Yet this was not even the best part of the parade.

Each year at the parade there was a competition that clowns could enter. I had won first place in this competition before, but earning that silky blue first-place ribbon meant so much more to me in my final parade. I was honored to be celebrated in that way, and I still have the ribbon as a memory of the great appreciation I have for the Lord's work in my life.

While in the white convertible, we sat in the lineup, waiting for the parade to start. People started coming up to the car and thanking me for the joy, happiness, hope, and love that I shared with everyone through the years. I was shocked! There were teenagers and young adults thanking me for the memories that I made and all of the work I had done. Then they leaned in and hugged me before running back to their place in the crowd. I thought that their kindness then was overwhelming, but that was just the beginning. When our convertible pulled forward, I was not prepared for what happened next.

The crowd stood up and burst into applause and cheers when we came into view. Many yelled that they loved me, and many more thanked me for my time as Sparkle and the love I shared with so many.

Tears streamed down both my cheeks as I heard these words. I had sacrificed a lot over the years with my time, finances, friends, and family to be Sparkle. To really be seen and appreciated for that sacrifice was beautifully humbling. The Lord let me receive all the love that I had shared with others on that ride.

This happened all the way through the parade. Any time we turned a corner or pulled onto a new street, people would stand and cheer, shouting their thanks and love. Everyone showed so much respect to me.

Whenever the car stopped, kids ran up and grabbed my hand. "We love you, Sparkle. Thank you for everything."

These were kids I had seen grow up since they were infants. My heart was overwhelmed, and I cried my gratitude.

Toward the end of the parade, I heard a beautifully familiar voice call out "Sparkle."

I turned quickly but missed him in the crowd. The car was moving, but I looked back and waved towards where I heard his voice. I knew it was a very dear friend of mine, Bob. Everyone called him "Mr. Mom". He was a single parent who raised his three kids by himself: Amber, Ashley, and Tyler.

One of the first times that I met him was at the Walla Walla Air Show, and it was Amber's first birthday. I was Sparkle at that event, and we took a picture together. Every year after that, Amber and I got a picture together on her birthday. Mr. Mom was a fantastic photographer, and he would show up at my work and bring me pictures that he had taken of me and Amber. Our annual birthday pictures continued every year until Amber started college, where she went off to become an incredible nurse.

Ashley is Amber's sister. She is also an amazing young woman. Ashley followed in her big sister's footsteps and joined the nursing program while working as a medical aide.

Tyler (TJ) is the youngest child. He has a heart that is full of love for everyone. Mr. Mom did an incredible job raising his children. He is a kindhearted, joyful, and positive man. Years ago, he became ill and his body started deteriorating. Mr. Mom eventually had to use a walker or wheelchair everywhere he went.

So you see, he and I were good friends.

Now picture this: Mr. Mom knew this was the last parade I was going to be in. He walked two miles with his walker to set up his camera at the end of the event so he could take a picture of my last parade. Imagine walking two miles with a walker, WOW!

Mr. Mom always visited me at the bank. After the parade, he came in and said, "Oooh my girl. I need a hug."

I walked around my teller station to give him a hug. Then he showed me the picture from the parade. It was me turned around, waving in his direction with a huge smile on my face from atop the convertible's seats. I still cherish that picture from my last parade.

As usual, I could not waste my time as Sparkle on just one event. After the parade, I went to the hospital to visit with people. I went from room to room visiting the patients and their families. I was so tired, but in my heart I kept feeling like I was supposed to go to another floor. I said, "Okay Lord."

When I got off the elevator, several people were sitting in the waiting room. I went over to visit with them. Since there were not any kids nearby, I felt that the Lord was pressing on my heart to just be real with them. This was where He wanted me to be, and He wanted me to listen if anyone wanted to talk.

I asked how everyone was doing, and they said not good. Their family member was passing away. To some he was their father, their grandfather, their brother or their husband. The family was there to say goodbye. I sat with them until the nurse said it was time and they could all go in. Before they did, I was able to give all of them a hug, and we prayed together.

Now I could leave and go home. My work as Sparkle was finished.

Almost.

We all live with the objective of being happy: our lives are all different and yet the same. –Anne Frank

CHAPTER 24

My Final Goodbye as Sparkle

While my final parade was a cherished and memorable event, my last event as Sparkle was filled with even more wonderful gifts and surprises.

As I look back on that magical day, I can still see and feel everything that I felt that day.

It was nearly six years ago, in October of 2019. I normally did not dress-up as Sparkle on Halloween, but this was an exception.

The Walla Walla Downtown Foundation wanted to do something special for me as a goodbye to Sparkle. They had a spot set up for people to get their pictures taken with Sparkle, and since it was Halloween, there would be a lot of kids dressed up in their costumes as well.

That morning I prayed to the Lord and asked Him to bless this day and pour His love onto me, so that I could share it with everyone I would come into contact with that day.

I prayed, "Let Your words be my words and Your touch be my touch so that everyone would feel Your presence and hear Your voice. Let me give encouragement where it is needed, hope to the hurting, and peace to the ones filled with anxiety and stress. Let them know they are not alone. Above all, please fill me with an outpouring of love for everyone. If there is someone special that You want me to see, then please show me who it is. Amen."

I wept through the whole prayer. This was the last time Sparkle would be able to bless people, and I wanted to make it count.

I also prayed for peace for myself. I was anxious and sad for my last appearance as Sparkle. I hoped to make it a magical day for everyone and to reach as many people as possible.

When I finished getting dressed as Sparkle, I went into my bedroom, knelt down, and prayed again. I told the Lord that this day was for Him, and this was His day. I was just his instrument. I also prayed that I would give out more *I Hugged A Clown Today!* stickers than ever before. I asked to be a blessing to people who might need encouragement today.

I was so excited to go out as Sparkle again, and my husband grinned when he saw me walk down the stairs. It was such a blessing to be able to appear as Sparkle one last time.

The downtown foundation event would not be until late afternoon, so I planned on visiting as many places as possible before the festivities started.

Around 8:45 a.m., I arrived at my first stop, Gesa Credit Union (where I worked). The theme at the office was *The Nightmare Before Christmas*. All of the staff were dressed up in creative and spooky costumes, and we took pictures together. We had so much fun hanging out, and then we opened the doors for locals to come through.

I took pictures with some of the members of Gesa, made balloon animals for kids, and enjoyed talking to guests. Then a man came up to me who I recognized, Heather's husband!

Heather was one of the special children I mentioned earlier in the story, who I met when she was four years old and had physical disabilities. We stayed close for all of those years, and Heather was hoping to see me on my last day.

Her husband, Kevin, showed me where they were parked. The car was not facing the building, so when I reached the passenger side, Heather looked up in surprise, a huge smile breaking out across her face. She threw open the car door so we could talk and hug. I was so excited to see her and say goodbye as Sparkle. She thanked me for all of my support and friendship over the years. I told her I was still there for her as Cindy.

We got a picture together, and I gave her another *I Hugged A Clown Today!* sticker. She had dozens of them from over the years, and I smiled giving her one more.

I felt so blessed to see Heather and all of the people at Gesa. It was an amazing start to the morning, and I thanked the Lord.

My second stop was Rogers Elementary School. I love Rogers because every year for about six or seven years, I did the school carnival for the kindergarteners that were going to be starting out in the fall. Since I only had time to visit one school, that was the one I picked.

When I got there it was lunchtime. They let me go in to speak with the first group that was eating lunch and tell them goodbye as Sparkle.

The kids were surprised and delighted when I walked into the cafeteria. I planned on starting at the closest table and walking around, but a little girl ran straight up to me. Other kids ran forward as well, leaving their lunches and reaching for a hug.

The little girl that stopped me (she was taller than I was) said, "Can I ask you a question?"

"Yes, of course!"

"Are you the *real* Sparkle?"

Children have asked me that before, because there were other people who dressed up as Sparkle around town, trying to impersonate me.

I met her eyes with a smile. "Yes, I am."

She gasped. "You were at my first birthday party. And you worked with my grandma at Baker Boyer Bank."

Then she turned around and yelled, "She's the real Sparkle!"

After that, I was bombarded with kids. The staff and I had to usher the kids to their seats, and I promised them that I would walk around and see everyone. I gave a hug (and sticker) to all of the kids there. They left when they finished eating, and then the second group came in.

They were also surprised to see a clown in the cafeteria, but this time the kitchen staff told the kids to sit down and I would walk around to talk with all of them.

Once the kids were seated, I said, "For those of you who don't know me, my name is Sparkle the Clown. I've come today to give out hugs, high fives, and my *I Hugged A Clown Today!* stickers."

The kids clamored for me to visit each of them. I made my way around to everyone so that no child was left out.

This happened with another group or two of students, and each time was just as precious as the first. I gave out a couple hundred stickers. Before leaving the cafeteria, I thanked the kitchen staff and gave stickers to everyone there.

Then I went to find a few of the special teachers that helped out when I clowned at the carnivals. I wanted to say a special goodbye to them, give a hug and sticker, and share how much I appreciated their love and support throughout the years. There was one teacher in particular that I wanted to see. I needed to tell her how much I appreciated her and all she did for Sparkle. This teacher got me hired for the carnival at the preschool and younger elementary school. One of my favorite events was welcoming kindergarteners before their first day of school.

I asked for Mrs. Schaffer. When I found her, I told her that this was my last day of being Sparkle because I had to stop for health reasons. We hugged, and I told her how much her friendship and support has meant to me over the years. I also told her that my goal was to give out more *I Hugged A Clown Today!* stickers than I ever had in one day. She believed I could!

Next I went to Regency at the Park, a rehabilitation center for physical therapy and long-term patient care. I spent a lot of time inside their facility as a patient when I had knee replacement surgery in 2014 and 2015. I have always had fond memories of Regency at the Park, so I was excited to go there and spend my time thanking nurses and visiting with patients. It was a special way to spend an hour of my afternoon.

My lovely friend Beth is a hairstylist, and she always makes people feel joyful and alive. She is a beautiful and kindhearted person. I stopped by to visit her but then ended up sharing my mixed emotions of the day. I was so joyful to be visiting and sharing love with so many people and having so many people hug and appreciate me. I also felt deeply saddened visiting people, knowing that it was the last time Sparkle would ever touch these people's lives.

Beth gave me a warm hug and reminded me of the beautiful things that Sparkle did for every person I met. She told me to go out and have fun. It was a day to celebrate all that Sparkle had done and to enjoy my time as Sparkle.

Talking to her made me feel better. I was ready to tackle the last and final part of my day. I was to attend Goodbye Pictures with Sparkle. There was a booth set up downtown where I could take pictures with kids as they walked around in their costumes.

When I arrived, kids were already standing in line to have their picture taken with me. The downtown area was packed. Parents walked with their kids to see Sparkle and trick-or-treat. My daughter Jenni showed up to give her mom, as well as Sparkle, a very special hug.

Jenni told me that she was so proud of me as both her mom and Sparkle. She asked how I was holding up, and I said that I was good, but I was getting tired.

Then I looked up, and there was my husband, Lew. He had a big smile on his face. He also asked how I was holding up, and I said really good. I was getting tired, but I also was having so much fun. Lew let me know that he was so proud of me as well. It warmed my heart to see Jenni and Lew, and their support on my last night as Sparkle meant everything to me.

Mr. Mom found me next. I gave him a big hug and his sticker. He took a few pictures of Sparkle, and then he took pictures of me and my husband and daughter all together.

I was amazed by all of the people who were downtown. I gave out hundreds of *I Hugged A Clown Today!* stickers. Some people came from Portland and Spokane just to tell Sparkle goodbye and what a difference I made in their life.

One young woman came from Spokane (three hours away) with her little baby girl just to see me again and tell me goodbye. She told me that when she was a little girl, she was afraid of clowns, but when she saw me and finally came up to meet me, she said that I was kind and loving. When I gave her a hug and one of my stickers, she was no longer afraid because she saw how kind I was. She also told me that she still has the same sticker I gave her all those years ago. Now she wanted me to give her baby girl a hug so that she can have a *I Hugged A Clown Today!* sticker too. She wanted to put her daughter's sticker next to her own in a scrapbook they shared together.

There were so many stories like hers that I got to experience that evening. People locally from Walla Walla and people from far away came to see Sparkle, take a picture, and get the famous hug and sticker. I was overwhelmed and blessed by the kindness shown to me by so many people.

Throughout the evening, I walked around and visited with parents and their kids. While I was out, I saw two scary clowns walking along the sidewalk. They looked to be in their late teens. I hurried to catch up with them. They were tall and wore their face paint in a grotesque manner. Cheerily I said, "Hi," and they said, "Hi back." I gained some courage and asked, "Can I have a hug so I can give you an *I Hugged A Clown Today*! sticker?"

One of the teenage boys eagerly said yes, while the other said no. The one who said yes let me give him a hug, but he refused my sticker. Then they asked me to join their side, the side of the scary clowns.

I confidently said no. My side is much better.

The scary clowns left after that, continuing down the sidewalk. I don't know if I made a difference in the one scary clown's heart, but I would like to believe that a little light touched his heart, and maybe, down the road, he will remember that someone cared about him.

Near the end of the event, I was exhausted. I was out from about 8:45 a.m. to 6:00 p.m. that last day. I saw so many people and was ready to go home.

When I got in my car, a few tears slid down my cheeks. I was so grateful for the day, even though it was long and I was emotionally and physically tired.

Once home, I went upstairs to my bedroom and closed the door. Then I knelt down to pray. I stayed on my knees in my Sparkle outfit, from my gloves to my glittery shoes, praying to the Lord.

I thanked the Lord for allowing me to be a part of His big plan by being Sparkle, all while tears streamed down my face. While I was praying to the Lord, I had my clown bag upstairs with me, and I felt Him tell me to check my bag.

When I opened the bag, I realized that I gave out between 700 and 800 *I Hugged A Clown Today*! stickers. A new flood of tears washed over me. The Lord had answered my prayer! It was a miracle that I gave out between 700-800.

The most that I ever gave out before that day was around 500.

The Lord is so amazing. There are so many beautiful gifts that He has given me through Sparkle. I just stand in awe!

Then I got up from my knees and took off my shoes, gloves, costume, and wig. I went through the very long process of taking the makeup off of my face. The process was concluded with a hot shower. I put on my pajamas, hugged my husband, ate a bite, drank lots of water, sat on the couch, and relaxed.

I decided I would put my stuff away tomorrow.

Just one positive thought in the morning can change your whole day! -Dalai Lama

CHAPTER 25

The Purple Plastic Tote Container

I decided that since I was going to be putting all of my Sparkle stuff away, I wanted to get a nice plastic tote that was fitting for Sparkle.

I looked at many different stores, but I could not find anything that would work. There were plain totes and blue ones, but none of them screamed "Sparkle!" I kept looking.

Several days later, I was in Walmart and continued my search for a plastic tote. Then I saw it, a beautiful violet tote that I would be able to store all of Sparkle's things inside. The best part was that it had a pink unicorn on the lid, and underneath, in beautiful script, it said, Believe in Magic.

The tote looked like the twilight sky. The colors were interwoven with deep pinks, blues, yellows, and mint greens. White stars glittered all over it.

This was my tote.

I realized that this was another gift from God. I looked all over to see if I could find another one, but there were no others to be found. I even looked in the kids' section of the store, but there was nothing.

When I took the violet tote up to the register, the clerk said "Wow, that sure is a pretty one! I haven't seen that before."

I smiled because I knew where it came from. It was a wonderful gift from God.

I paid and walked out of the store with a big smile on my face. When I got home, I shared this story with my husband, about how the Lord gave me another gift.

Later that day, as I gently packed away Sparkle's costume, I had a thankful heart and tears in my eyes.

"All our dreams can come true, if we have the courage to pursue them." -Walt Disney

CHAPTER 26

The Dress That Did Not Fit

Five years after my last event as Sparkle, my husband and I took a trip to Republic, Washington. Lew grew up in Republic, and we still have the cabin where he was raised. He was even born in that cabin.

That cabin is where we stay when we have the chance. Republic is a beautiful little area, reminiscent of *Little House On The Prairie*. The slow-paced town is tucked into the mountains, surrounded by tall pines and on a crystal blue lake.

Republic is in the top right-hand corner of the state next to the Canadian border. We have good friends that live up there, and we visit them every time we go up.

One of my very special friends who I love to visit is Kellie. We have been close for many years. Kellie is a young mother of two. Her three-year-old boy is vibrant and excitable, loving life. Her five month old is a sweet, snuggly baby girl.

When we stopped by in 2025 to say hi, one of Kellie's closest friends, Mae, was there as well. Mae was an incredible person and friend, and we all laughed a lot. She was very kind and asked a lot of questions about my life and the book that I was working on describing my time as Sparkle.

Kellie then made an offer. She is a professional photographer, and she said that she would come down to Walla Walla and take professional pictures of Sparkle putting on her outfit and makeup. It was a special gift from Kellie to me. Because of the gift that Sparkle gave to others, she wanted to give me a gift in return.

I was a little nervous to accept her offer. Not many people had seen me get ready as Sparkle. It was a vulnerable process, doing my hair and makeup with deliberate, practiced motions to transform into Sparkle. Also, it had been five years since I had put on my outfit. Yet the more I thought about it, the more excited I got. I told Kellie that I would love to be Sparkle again, even if for a short time. She planned on coming to Walla Walla a month and a half later.

Three weeks before Kellie came down, I asked my husband to bring down my tote. When I opened the box, I became overwhelmed with excitement. I had so much fun looking at all of my treasures, but oh my. When I laid out all of my dresses, my pink shoes, and the wig, the impact of what Sparkle had done over the years overwhelmed me.

I put away my pink shoes, because I did not want to see them all the time. They were magical to me, and the way that I looked at it, Sparkle's pink shoes would be the finishing touch to her outfit.

I decided that Sparkle deserved a new wig because I had worn that one for about eight or nine years. I wanted one that was bright and new, just like Sparkle always was for others. I put a rush order on the wig and new makeup so it would arrive in time. When the new wig got to my house, the material was high quality and the style was cute with pink bangs. The wig took me five hours to style. I cut layers to the bangs and added glitter and jewels. It took so long to work on that I did not even try on the wig beforehand.

After I took everything out of the tote, the one thing that I kept out was my dress. I hung it up and kept looking at it. Every time I passed my dress, I would touch it.

Each dress that I wore over the years was uniquely personal and memorable. I loved each of them because they were made at different times by different people, which were perfect for that occasion. The first dress I wore for seven years. The second dress I wore for ten years, and this last one I wore for almost ten years as well. Yet there was something about this final one, this pink sparkly dress that held all my lasts, that I loved the most.

One morning, my husband said to me, "You won't be able to wear the dress. It won't fit you the way it should."

He said it would not fit because of how crooked my back is now. My spine is coming down on my heart and lungs, which widens the top half of my back and chest area. I went from being four foot eight inches to four foot six inches. I was upset by his comment and told him, "Yes, I can fit in it."

When Lew was not around, I ran upstairs and quickly tried on the dress. Guess what? I could not fit in it. Because my back was all out of sorts, the dress would not zip up past the bottom portion of my back. I wanted to cry, but decided I would take off my dress and hang it up again in the bedroom. I chose not to say anything to my husband because I hoped it was not true. Perhaps the next time I tried it on, the dress would zip up all the way. A day and a half went by, and I tried on the dress again. This time I asked my husband to help me zip it up. It only zipped up to the lower portion of my back. Lew said, "I am so sorry Cindy, but it won't fit because your spine is too crooked."

I did cry this time. Each time I passed the dress over the next couple of days, I reached up and touched it. Then a few days later I tried the dress on a third time, and again it did not fit. Where the dress stopped, the zipper came up to the midsection of my back, it was like a "V." There was absolutely no way that I could fit into this dress.

This time I truly broke down and cried because I knew it was not going to fit.

I cried so much because I knew Sparkle really was over. Kellie was coming in a little over a week, and my grief lasted the whole time until she and Mae arrived. I even called Lynn, my friend who made the dress for me. When Lynn and I talked, I realized that there was nothing she could do to fix the dress in time for the pictures.

A friend gave me an idea: once my face was all made up, I should put on my wig and gloves. Since I would already have on my tights, socks and white bathrobe, I would be ready except for my shoes. Then Kellie could take pictures of me reaching up for my dress. This was the best that we could do under the circumstances. It was important for me to have my dress in the pictures, even if I could not wear it.

Kellie and Mae got in Friday night, and began setting up for our photo shoot.

Saturday afternoon, we were at a hotel to get ready and take pictures. I started the whole process of getting made up. Kellie laid out all of my accessories so she could take pictures. It was so much fun getting ready, and by the end

I felt so excited because Sparkle was almost back. When Kellie was taking pictures of me reaching for my dress, I felt this electricity go through me. I thought it was because I was cold. Kellie kept taking pictures of me as I walked about the room and looked in the mirror. Then she said, "Do you trust me?"

"Yes," I said, without a doubt.

"Would you please put on the dress one more time?"

"Okay," I said, "but it won't zip up."

"Let's just do it one more time," Kellie said.

First we put on the petticoat skirt. I took a deep breath and thought, "Here we go."

As we stood in front of the mirror, Kellie started zipping up my dress, but she did not stop. She zipped it up all the way to my neck!

I cried and cried. It was impossible to believe that my dress zipped up all the way. I praised the Lord with all of my heart and soul. Kellie and Mae helped me get situated, and then we left. We needed to stop by my house. Somehow, I had also forgotten my rainbow eyelashes and sparkles for my face. Yet I think that the Lord had another reason for me to go back home. My husband needed to witness this miracle of the "Pink Dress" as much as we all needed to witness it. The look on Lew's face was priceless when we stepped into the house. There was no doubt that the Lord had His hands holding me, with my beautiful pink dress on. There are many times in the Bible where the number three is referenced as a holy number. The Holy Trinity is made of God, Jesus, and the Holy Spirit. Jesus rose from the dead on the third day. After three failed attempts for my dress to fit, it finally did. I knew the Lord blessed me that afternoon.

What amazes me is how the Lord is always making what seems "impossible become possible," even in the smallest details of one's life. He is always showing His love for us in one way or another.

Life is not about waiting for the storm to pass by, but learning to dance in the rain.

CHAPTER 27

My Letter to Sparkle

Dear Sparkle,

I have so much to say to you, but I really don't know where to begin. Do I just tell you thank you? That answer is easy for me to answer… because it's NO.

You have shown and taught me so much.

You taught me how to truly show compassion and love in a world that wants to hate others. When you saw hurting people, you always went straight to them. You let them know that they were safe, valued, and loved so very much. You shared that the Lord loved them, and you loved them with all your heart as well.

You sat and listened while people talked, letting them know that they were heard. Then you shared with each and every person that they are so loved and valued, just as they are. You were a wonderful light, always showing compassion and, above all, love.

Sparkle, you always loved everyone no matter what. You took people at their worst and truly showed them what unconditional love was like.

You even showed love to the people who wandered the streets, who looked like they hadn't bathed in weeks, and who spoke out loud to themselves. It didn't matter to you because the Lord was teaching you boldness and to trust Him. He was with you and He would protect you! Sure enough, you would walk over and talk to them and listen to what they had to say. By the end, they were calm, and you would ask, "Can I give you a hug? I have these *I Hugged A Clown Today*! stickers and I have to do what it says." Then they would say yes, and you would give them a hug and sticker. They always went away happy.

It was so important for you to always be authentic and honest with everyone. You never changed your voice because you wanted everyone, including the children, to know that you were real and not fake, that the person underneath the clothing, wig and makeup was a real person who truly loved all of them.

I watched as you talked with kids that were just trying to fit in, but felt they couldn't because of a physical challenge. As they cried, you felt their tears as well. You let them know that it was okay to cry because that was a true feeling. Then you told them your story. You shared how when you were born, you had cerebral palsy but learned to walk. At a young age, you were in a horse riding accident where you were in a coma for nineteen days and became totally paralyzed on the right side of your body. The doctors thought that you would never walk again, but how you proved those doctors wrong.

You gave the person that you were talking to hope, and everyone needs hope.

When you noticed the deaf standing back because they felt most people couldn't communicate with them, you took a couple of sign language classes so you could speak with them. That made them feel included and not left out. You definitely put smiles on their faces.

You taught me how to be fearless and strong while knowing that I was always protected by the One who truly loves us all.

You taught me what the true meaning of integrity and authenticity was. You stood on the positive values that you carried and did not let anyone change you.

At times I saw how hard it was for you because you would have rather been home with your family. You hoped and prayed that your kids truly understood what you were trying to accomplish while out there helping others.

I feel so honored and blessed to have been a part of the Lord's plan with you, Sparkle, for thirty-five years. You have given me so much joy and happiness through the years.

While I thought your wider purpose ended many years ago, after your final event, I have come to realize that you are still making an impact. This book, full of stories of courage and compassion, is your legacy now. You show my children how much I love them and just how much I appreciate the sacrifices they made. You show courage and give inspiration to readers on the edge of pursuing their own dreams. You remind the readers that they too are loved. They too get to be touched by the magic of Sparkle, all these years later.

Now I am lying in my bed praying to the Lord, asking Him to help me as "Cindy" to continue to hold on to the values that you have instilled in me in my everyday life.

You showed me the value of being authentic and standing tall so others can see the integrity I carry. You tell me to give all people hope, because we all need it! You remind me to be fearless and strong, knowing that I am not alone.

I love and thank you for everything.

With loving thoughts,
Cindy

FREE
FREE
HUG COUPON
Good For One Hug. Redeemable
From Any Participating Human Being
FREE
FREE

Sparkle's Tool Box

I have created Sparkle's Tool Box as a resource for people who are inspired by Sparkle and want ideas on how to share hope and love with their family, friends and community.

I thought long and hard about what gifts I could share with you, my wonderful readers. I created a couple of sections that you can read through based on your own time, resources, and investment into using some of Sparkle's tricks.

So my lovely readers, I want you all to feel my love by letting me share a few of my very best messages and ideas with you!

Remember: you don't have to dress up as a clown to touch someone's life in a positive way, just be YOU. Search your heart and you will know what to do and what to say.

Magic Tricks

I decided on three magic tricks that meant so much to me when I wanted to give a powerful message. I performed them with sleight of hand magic for thirty-five years. These messages gave hope, peace, healing, and love to all who heard them.

The Needle and the Balloon

Props:

15" sharp needle with an eye
Thread thin enough to go through the needle
Vegetable oil or petroleum jelly
Cloth
Balloon
Glitter (optional)

Prep:

Put the vegetable oil on the cloth.
Put glitter in the balloon you are going to use.

Activity:

I usually get a couple of big, strong guys to come up on stage, and I ask them to pick a balloon (which I have several for them to choose from). Then I tell them to blow up the balloon as big or as small as they would like because we are going to put a needle through the balloon, and I will do the same.

Once we blow up our balloons, I tell the boys to stick the needle through their balloon without popping it.

Of course their balloons pop, and then it is my turn.

I rub my cloth up and down the needle, which already has the thread tied to it. As I give my message on being prepared in life, I tell the audience that I have a little bit of vegetable oil on my cloth, and that I am prepared to help the needle have the highest likelihood of not popping the balloon. I joke with them that my balloon is smaller because my hands are smaller and I need to hold the balloon (but it is also easier to do with a smaller balloon).

It is easiest to put the needle through the bottom of the balloon, close to where the knot is and where the latex is thickest.

As I put the needle through the balloon, I stress to the crowd the importance of being prepared in life. Depending on my audience, I give different examples of how they can be prepared. If I am with children, I tell them they can work hard in school. They can study to prepare for tests. They can attend sports practices to be ready on game day.

My advice to you is to use your own words and make it your own. That is the only way that your message will be authentic to your listeners, if you speak from your heart!

While I am talking, I slowly put the needle through the balloon so it comes out of the opposite side, with the thread going through too. The audience is always so impressed that it works. Then I pop the balloon, letting glitter shower onto the stage to show that it was a real balloon – This is always a great message for kids but could work in other environments as well.

The Polka-Dotted Scarves

Props:

A change/switch bag (from a magic store/website)
A small bag of white hole-punched paper
A small bag of blue hole-punched paper
A magic wand

1 white scarf
1 blue scarf
1 white scarf with blue polka dots
1 blue scarf with white polka dots
(I usually make my scarves out of fabric from a craft store)

Prep:

Put the polka-dotted scarves in the secret compartment of the switch bag.
Combine the white hole-punched paper with the blue hole-punched paper in a clear bag.

Activity:

I have three volunteers come forward. I give one a white scarf, one a blue scarf, and the third my magic wand.

I pick up my bag and show the audience that it is empty. Then I ask the two volunteers with the scarves to put them in my bag. I tell the audience that the scarves are going to magically change. I then have the third person tap my bag three times with my wand. Each time they need to say my special phrase really loud (I usually choose "twinkle toes").

When the volunteers reach into the bag and pull out the scarves, the audience says that the scarves did not change. I say yes they did...the white scarf is now blue, and the blue one is now white. The audience laughs and groans, so then I say that we will do something different with the scarves.

The volunteers are told to put their scarves back in the bag. I give the volunteer with the wand a little bag filled with blue and white hole-punched paper. I tell the volunteer to dump all of the dots in my bag and pick up the wand. I have the volunteer with the wand say, "twinkle toes" three times. When they check the bag, they discover that the scarves and paper dots look the same.

The solution is for all three volunteers (and sometimes the audience too) to say "twinkle toes" really loud.

I egg them on to say it louder and louder. While they do this, I switch the opening to the other side of the bag, where the polka-dotted scarves are. When they finally shout it loud enough, I tell the volunteers to reach in and pull out the scarves. White polka dots are now on the blue scarf and blue polka dots are on the white scarf. They look in my bag and find that the loose, paper polka dots are gone.

I use this trick to tell the audience how wonderful it is that every single one of us changes every day. For kids, I say that they are growing more beautiful and handsome every day, not to mention taller as well. I tell the audience that there are some days they wake up and feel mad and have a bad attitude towards everyone. Yet they have a choice – to stay mad or to be happy. I find that when I am helping someone and take the focus off of me, I become happier.

There are always opportunities to change one's attitude and help others. I give examples like visiting someone who broke their leg, helping a friend study, setting the table for dinner, or doing dishes without complaining.

It all starts with choosing to change your attitude.

Next time you see a couple of scarves, remember this message and know, "Only you can change your attitude."

Torn Heart

What is special about this trick is that it is incredibly impactful for kids and adults. It is my favorite one to do.

Props:

2 identical pink paper hearts

Activity:

In one hand, carefully crumpled into my palm, is one of the hearts that I do not let the audience see. I hold up the other pink heart and say, "What is this?"

The audience says that it is a heart and I respond, "It's not just any heart, it symbolizes our heart." Then I say, "There are things every day that happen to us. Some days your heart feels this big."

I hold up the whole, full heart.

"Then there are other days that it doesn't work out. Maybe you are getting a divorce." I rip the heart, and continue tearing it into smaller pieces as I give more examples.

"Maybe you are struggling at work, or you've lost a loved one. Maybe recovery has been more difficult than you anticipated."

With kids I usually say, "Some days we get up and our hearts feel this big, and everything is going great. But then things happen to us that are out of our control. Maybe you studied really hard for a big test that you needed to pass, but you blew it. Maybe your pet died. Maybe your parents are going through a divorce and that tears at your heart."

At this point, I have shredded scraps of paper in my hands.

"But when you have been touched by someone who really loves you and cares about you, like your parents, a special teacher, grandparents, or good friends." Here I stop and hold out my hands with the torn heart inside for the audience to see and touch the shredded pieces. "Then it allows the Lord to come into our heart and work miracles."

I remind them of the torn heart, but also how the Lord can heal their broken heart. While I am talking, I squish the scraps into a tight ball. Then it is time to reveal the full heart. As I am unraveling the full heart from my palm, the audience is focused on the new heart. They do not notice when I slip the shredded pieces of paper into my pocket with my other hand.

I open my hands to reveal a whole heart that was put back together.

"When the Lord is inside you, then you can be made whole."

Look for Slydini Tear - Torn & Restored Newspaper Trick - Explained Step by Step on You Tube.

Simple Blessings

There are easy ways to engage with an audience or someone who is hurting by just using a few consistent easy props. Here are some of my favorites:

BOOKS

There are a lot of children's books with good morals that can be read at birthday parties, schools, or even to adults in hospitals or recovery. Here are some of my favorites:

The Whistling Frog from Lily Pad Pond, by William Crain, illustrated by Brian Crain.
Adventures of the Little Green Dragon, by Mari Privette Ulmer, illustrated by Mary Maass.

Henrietta the Homely Duckling, by Phil Hahn, illustrated by Paul Coker Jr.

NOTES

An encouraging word can go a long way in impacting someone's day. Here are ideas for little cards or notes to have on hand:

A free hug/smile coupon

Stickers that say, "I love you!"

An encouraging Bible verse or quote on a note card.

A SMALL GIFT

Sometimes a tangible take-away is a gift that people can use to not necessarily remember you by, but remember how you made them feel. Here are some of my favorite and easiest gifts to have with me in group settings:

Balloons for balloon animals

Baked goods

Coloring pages and crayons

The Simplest Blessing

More than any magic tricks that I have done, or any gifts that have been given, I have found that the ability to show up and listen to someone has the greatest impact. You do not need items to truly make an impression. Just showing a kind and loving heart is enough.

You can visit:

Nursing homes

Hospitals

Someone who has lost a family member

Someone who is homebound
Someone who just had a baby
A neighbor, just to say hi

* * *

These magic tricks, presentations and intentional acts of kindness have touched so many hearts and souls. Messages of love can be shared with the young and old, the hurting, the sad, and the lost. They give hope to people. In reference to the great love and power of Christ, Philippians 4:13 (ESV) says, "I can do all things through him who strengthens me."

Our God is an amazing God. In Deuteronomy 31:6 (ESV) it says, "Be strong and courageous. Do not be afraid or terrified because of them, for the Lord your God goes with you; he will never leave you nor forsake you."

We are not alone. These messages of love and hope remind people of that. Christ will always be with them. This truth provides opportunities for healing that only the Lord can do, involving not just our bodies but our hearts, minds, and emotions as well. Christ loves you. He wants to be your best friend. He wants to be closer than a brother or sister to us. If other people (from around the world) shared these messages, then so many people could find healing, hope, peace, and above all, love.

REFERENCE PAGE

Types of Clowns

When someone says "clown" most people get the same mental image: a white-faced, tall man in a baggy, colorful outfit with huge shoes and a red ball nose. Many might think of the Ronald McDonald type of clown. However, there are actually six main types of clowns, each with their own unique style and attributes.

The Rodeo Clown

The rodeo clown is very specialized. As their name suggests, they often perform in arenas during rodeos and provide comic relief and entertainment. When there is a slow period in the rodeo events, they keep the audience entertained with funny antics. A rodeo clown is a performer who works in all of the events to keep the crowd and the participants safe. They are usually dressed in the "Auguste Clown" style and wear baggy attire with protective vests and pads underneath in case of an altercation with an animal.

The Tramp Clown / The Hobo Clown

The tramp clown was inspired by homeless people in the late nineteenth century. Their clothes are often ragged, torn, and patched. They wear less white makeup, and only use it around their eyes and mouth. They often have artificial beards using greasepaint that look sooty and give off a working-class feel. They perform a lot of physical comedy with exaggerated movements and endearing personas. Tramp clowns do not speak, but entertain audiences with humorous acts and playful jesting. One of the most famous tramp clowns is Emmett Kelly, also known as, "Hobo Kelly," who portrayed his hobo character as "Weary Willie". He was famous during the Great Depression, and thus portrayed a more sad character.

The Auguste Clown

The auguste clown is a very fun-loving, lighthearted, joyous clown. They like to be entertaining and, at times, mischievous. They are all about entertaining their audience with exaggerated expressions, slapstick comedy, and pranks of all sorts. They often have a flesh- or pink-colored face with white only around the eyes and mouth. They usually have a large red nose, wear gloves, sometimes with the fingertips cut out. Similar to rodeo clowns, they use baggy clothes and frequently show some skin on their arms and legs.

Mime Clown

The mime, or pantomime clown, is a clown that does dramatic performances in which a story is being told solely by expressive body movements. They first appeared in

Greece in the 5th century BC as comic entertainers. Staying true to their name, they do not speak but rather emphasize communication through physical movements, gestures, and facial expressions. They convey both happy and sad stories solely through their bodies and facial expressions. Usually mime clowns are dressed more monochromatically, in black or white attire.

The Classic White–Faced Clown

A classic white–faced clown features a full white face with defined features in contrasting colors (usually red, black, or blue). They often wear a traditional, colorful costume with a ruffled neck and a pointed hat. They are covered head to toe with no skin showing. To cover up completely they also wear gloves and tights. They are often a little more sophisticated and intelligent than one would expect, and have a little more class than other clowns. Their most important feature is their face, and they pay special attention to their makeup.

The Grotesque White–Faced Clown

The grotesque white–faced clown is similar to the classic but is a little zanier using more exaggerated features and clothes. They are a little brighter, bolder, and excessive. The most common examples include Bozo the Clown and Ronald McDonald, but they can range all the way to Batman's arch-nemesis, the Joker.

Acknowledgments

My heart is so full of gratitude to all of the many people who helped make this book evolve from a dream to reality!

First off, I would like to acknowledge and thank my Lord and Savior Jesus Christ for allowing me to be a part of this amazing ride. He was the conductor while I was a mere instrument!

To Brian Hernandez, owner of Mac Walla Walla: Thank you so much for helping me with my laptop so that I could have a good one on which to write my story. You were always there when I needed help, and I appreciate that so much!

Barbara Hemphill: I was so blessed the day that our paths ran smack into each other (literally speaking). You are an amazing, strong woman that I aspire to be like. That's not to mention what an incredible author and podcast speaker you are. Thank you for taking me under your wing!

Kevin White: The day that you told Barbara that you would like to talk to me was the day that brought my dreams to life. You said to me, "No one has ever done what you have done before. You need to write your story." You have given me strength and the belief that I can write my story, and that it will make a difference. Thank you for your belief in me!

Beverly LeMaster and Brittney Lerzo: Wow! What can I say, except that both of you are the best Angel Writers I could have ever asked for. Beverly, you were my first Angel Writer, and I learned so much from you. The way that you wrote had me amazed to see "my words" on paper. We had a wonderful time, and then you had to go and have your baby. You told me to trust Brittney, and I felt better about the exchange. Brittney, the way that you and I work together is amazing! I enjoy our initial writings and discussions of my story with you. Yet when you send it back to me: oh my gosh! It is everything that I could ask for and want. Ladies, I love you both so much.

Kellie Cook: you are an incredible young lady who drove 250 miles from your home by the Canadian border to bring tears of joy and happiness to my eyes. You are such an incredible photographer – one of the best that I have ever seen. Thank you so much. I will cherish those pictures forever.

Mae Wheaton: You are the wonderful friend that all of us want and need in our lives. You drove down with Kellie to help take care of her baby girl while she set up and took the pictures of me as Sparkle. You are so selfless and giving, filled with so much love, joy, peace, and happiness. I am so blessed to call you my friend.

Andrea Lowe: I have known you since you were in junior high with my daughter. Now you are a beautiful and positive young woman. A few years ago, when I saw you and your husband at the store, you were dressed up as a clown and looked so adorable. You told me how I inspired you to go for your dreams, being a balloonist as well as a photographer. That meant the world to me. You have a business, Connection Photography, and a wonderful partner, Sarah McBride. Thank you so much for taking my picture for the back cover of the book. You have no idea how much that means to me.

I would like to thank my beautiful friend, Tamila Sandberg, for all of her love, encouragement, and strength when I felt like quitting. You and I have developed a close friendship, and I just want you to know how much I have appreciated your smile during this whole process. Taya, I would like to thank you for helping me with my flyers. You did such a beautiful job taking my ideas and putting your amazing talent towards it to come up with a fun flyer. You have a real gift, my beautiful friend.

To all of my friends who work in the Cardio Rehab department at Providence St. Mary's Hospital: You all encouraged me to keep my body strong by exercising my muscles, especially around my spine. When I told all of you that I was going to be writing a book on my time as Sparkle, all the love and encouragement that you gave me made me feel like I could do this. So I want to thank all of you for this beautiful gift.

To my beautiful friend Peggy Waggoner: I really want to give you a big 'thank you!' for teaching me the basics of sign language so that I could speak with the deaf. What an incredible gift you gave me.

Cara Ellis, Linda Schaub, and Lynn Eckles: I would like to thank each one of you amazing women for believing in Sparkle and seeing my vision. Each of you beautiful ladies touched my heart in a very powerful way. You came into my life at just the right moment, and the outfits that each of you created were perfect. Cara, you were the one who made my first outfit, and it was so fun. I loved it and wore it for about nine years. Linda, as Sparkle matured you gave me my first princess dress. I felt so beautiful in it and wore that dress for over fifteen years. I absolutely loved it. Lynn, you have made the most incredible quilts that I have ever seen. When we started talking, I showed you pictures and told you all about who Sparkle was and the dream that was in my heart for Sparkle. You were very excited and wanted to help fulfill my dream. The dress was absolutely breathtaking, and again I felt like a revived princess. I want to say a special thank you to my Three Awesome Angels. I love you all so much.

Skeeter Gossett: You have always been a very good friend to both me and my husband. When I asked if I could ride on the back of your convertible, you did not hesitate. Especially since you knew that it was my last parade before retiring. You washed and waxed that car until it sparkled! It was the most beautiful car there, and YES we won a blue ribbon too! That was the most emotional parade I had ever been in, and I was so thankful to have you there to drive me and support me as my friend.

To my husband, Lew Sprengel: Thank you for showing up at the Noah's Ark graduation to see who the *real* Sparkle was and what she was all about. On that day, it seemed I changed how you looked at clowning, and since then you have always believed in Sparkle. You have shown up to every event that I have done. Thank you for always believing in me.

To my beloved daughter Jennifer Nakonieczny: I really want to thank you for all of your love and support throughout all the years of me being Sparkle. Now you have come alongside me again with this book. You encouraged me with my writing, right down to getting me a hot pink binder with sparkles on it filled with colored paper and vibrant pens to write down my ideas. You have shown up at every function Sparkle has done to just say, "I love you, and I am here." Thank you.

To all of my other friends and family across the state who have encouraged me and given me hope while writing this book: I want to thank you with all of my heart and soul. You have no idea the impact that you all have had on my life. May Sparkle's story continue to bring you hope and love when you think of her.

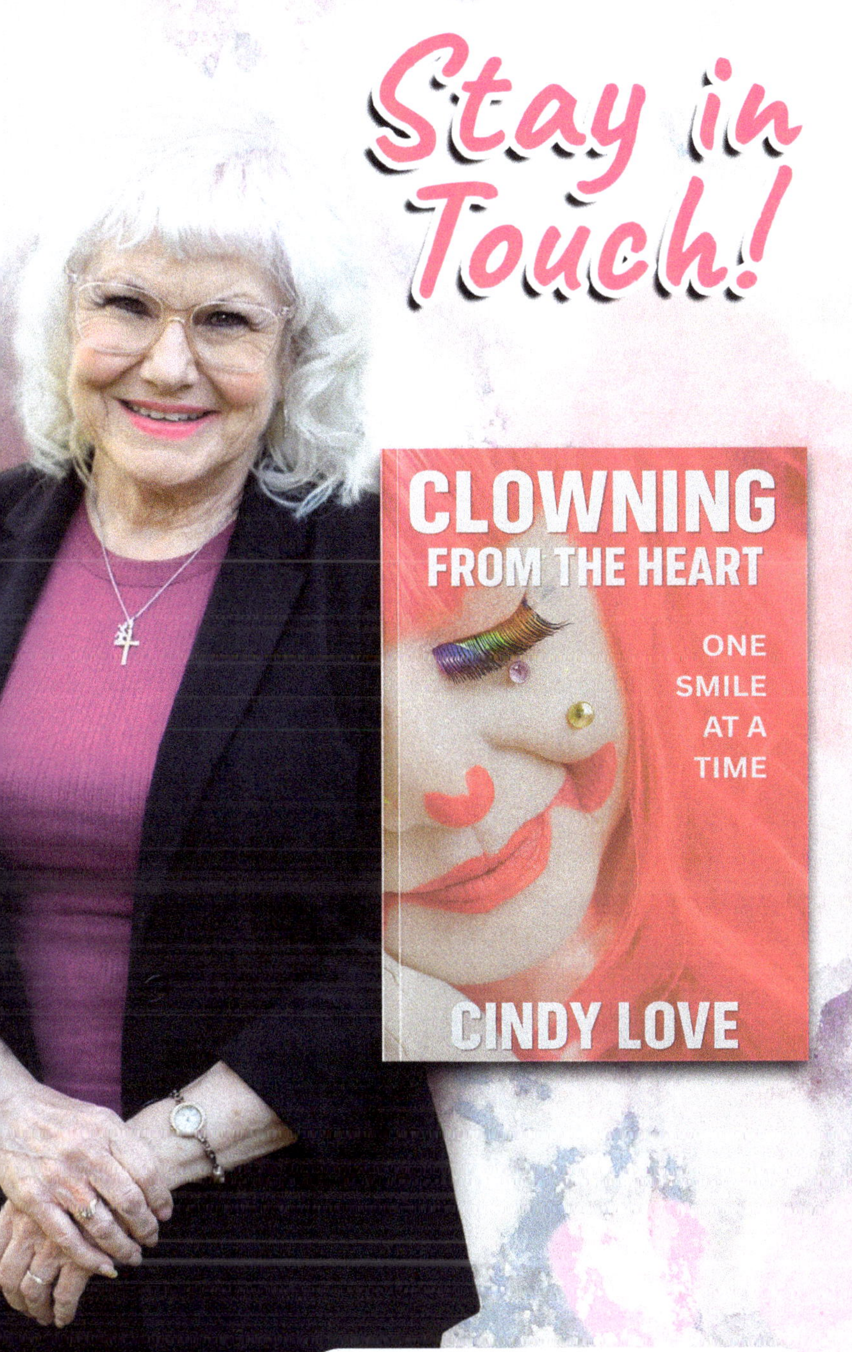
Stay in Touch!
CLOWNING
FROM THE HEART
ONE SMILE AT A TIME
CINDY LOVE

www.ingramcontent.com/pod-product-compliance
Ingram Content Group UK Ltd.
Pitfield, Milton Keynes, MK11 3LW, UK
UKHW021837270726
14058UKWH00002B/197